CHEERS FOR CATHY'S RESUME P
AND
CRAFTING A RESUME THAT LANDS YOU THE JOB

"Positioning yourself in the new competitive marketplace can be difficult. With profiles, posts, bios, and resumes, creating a unified bundle that highlights your expertise, experience, and value can be overwhelming. When I am looking to enhance my resume, bio, or practice interview questions, Cathy Posner is my first call. I have recommended Cathy and her services to professionals all over the country. Her experience and advice have helped people articulate their value and position for new levels of impact!"

JJ DiGeronimo
Speaker, Founder of Tech Savvy Women and Author of
Accelerate Your Impact: Action-Based Strategies to Pave Your Professional Path

"I trust Cathy Posner for her practical, hands-on approach to revising a resume. Cathy coaches and teaches you how to best represent your specific skills and talents. Because of Cathy's experience as a career transition specialist and coach, she is uniquely qualified to provide deep insight into resume structure, language use, and formatting. If you are looking to update your resume or take your materials up a notch, *Crafting a Resume that Lands You the Job* is the resource that you need!"

Connie Thackaberry
HR Manager, Coach, and Speaker working in the legal sector

"After 33 years in one industry—nearly 29 years with one company—it was time for change. I had no resume, was in need of an updated LinkedIn profile, and needed serious one-on-one coaching. Cathy created a powerful career and personal brand for me. In addition to coaching, I needed confidence, and Cathy provided both. From the beginning, Cathy asked very pointed and professional questions so that she could build and expand my materials. Cathy brought out my best talents with her written expression."

Former Client working as a
Chief Revenue Officer in media

"Cathy is the best resume writer I have worked with in my career. She is the consummate professional and has the gift of being able to take the daunting process of resume writing and make it simple and painless, even for someone who had not had to update her resume for many years. Cathy was able to convey my extensive experience, skill set, and story on paper. Her coaching and guidance was truly key to the amount of opportunities I received. I have recommended Cathy to multiple colleagues and will continue to do so in the future."

Former Client working as a
Vice President of Corporate Accounts in healthcare

"Cathy's work is insightful, creative, responsive, and detail-oriented. Her resume process is thorough, and she's a pleasure to work with. And the result is top-notch. A hiring partner told me, "This is the most professional resume I've ever seen."

Former Client working as a
mid-career Litigation Attorney

"Cathy is a true professional and honest businesswoman who drives value. I came away from our work with an entirely new perspective on how to deliver my work history. She guided me to relay the value of my previous experience in a way that allowed her to create a professional resume tailored just for me. I now have a resume that makes hiring managers and HR people take notice."

Former Client working as a
Cybersecurity Supervisor in the insurance industry

"I worked with Cathy as I was about to transition from college to post-college life. Cathy helped me to think about myself, my career, and future direction on an important level. She asked me the tough questions that helped me elevate my resume to showcase my best assets, as well as where I want to go. She helped translate my basic job history into a complete story that jumps off the page."

Former Client working as a
Senior Analyst in the senior housing industry

"I credit Cathy's Resume Refresh program for helping me transition from regional management into a Vice President of Sales position in the industrial business sector. She helped me to organize and wordsmith my resume and LinkedIn profile in a professional manner that made it more attractive to recruiters and business prospects. Through Cathy's coaching and direction, we reorganized my experience and qualifications in a manner more consistent with the executive positions I was seeking. I still receive compliments on how brilliantly organized my LinkedIn profile page is today."

Former Client working as a
Vice President in sales

"I began working with Cathy at a time when I was transitioning from an in-house research position to independent consulting. Cathy was able to help me reframe my professional and academic experiences to attract consulting clients and sell my work as a "small business." Cathy taught me to think about the various audiences who will view my resume and to ensure that I am conveying the most relevant information in a concise and manageable format."

Former Client working as a
Business Consultant in the evaluation and assessment industry

CRAFTING A RESUME THAT LANDS YOU THE JOB

A STEP-BY-STEP GUIDE TO WRITING A COMPELLING RESUME

CATHY POSNER

CRAFTING A RESUME THAT LANDS YOU THE JOB
A Step-by-Step Guide to Writing a Compelling Resume

Copyright © 2019 by Cathy Posner

All rights reserved. No part of this publication may be reproduced, distributed, or transmitted in any form or by any means, including photocopying, recording, or other electronic or mechanical methods, without the prior written permission of the author, except in the case of brief quotations embodied in critical reviews and certain other noncommercial uses permitted by copyright law. For permission requests contact the author.

Limit of Liability/Disclaimer of Warranty: The publisher and the author make no REPRESENTATIONS or warranties with respect to the accuracy or completeness of the contents of this work and specifically disclaim all warranties, including without limitation warranties of fitness for a particular purpose. No warranty may be created or extended by sales or promotional materials. The advice and strategies contained herein may not be suitable for every situation. This work is sold with the understanding that the publisher is not engaged in rendering legal, accounting, or other professional services. If professional assistance is required, the services of a competent professional person should be sought. Neither the publisher nor the author shall be liable for damages arising herefrom. The fact that an organization or website is referred to in this work as a citation and/or a potential source of further information does not mean that the author or the publisher endorses the information the organization or website may provide or recommendations it may make. Further, readers should be aware that internet websites listed in this work might have changed or disappeared between the time this work was written and the time it is read.

To contact Cathy:

Website	www.TransitionConsultingAndCoaching.com
Email	Cathy@TransitionConsultingAndCoaching.com
LinkedIn	www.linkedin.com/in/CathyPosner/
Facebook	@TransitionConsultingAndCoachingCathyPosner

To contact the publisher, inCredible Messages Press, visit www.inCredibleMessages.com.

Printed in the United States of America
ISBN 978-1-7322510-5-2

Book Strategist & Editor	Bonnie Budzowski	inCredible Messages
Cover Design	Bobbie Fox Fratangelo	Bobbie Fox Inc.
Author Photographer	Lisa Pflaum Saunders	Lisa Pflaum Photography

DEDICATION

To Mason and Lucinda: always supportive and willing to play my reindeer games. You are my North Star.

To my clients of the last decade plus: I recently came across this quote by Brené Brown to share with you: "Let go of who you think you're supposed to be; embrace who you are." Your professional stories inspire me daily. Keep telling them proudly!

Contents

CHAPTER 1

PREPPING THE CANVAS

We live in an interesting culture. We accelerate and achieve in our careers based on accomplishments, but we are taught from a young age to be hesitant about sharing our accomplishments. Were you ever told not to brag? Conflicting ideas, right?

A resume is one of the places you can brag about yourself. No one else, except possibly your mother, is going to do that for you. In fact, let's not call it "bragging." Let's call it sharing the good story of you.

"Writing about my professional history is fun!" said no one ever. In fact, the proposition of that task is often greeted with fear, loathing, and anxiety. Everyone has self-doubt about how he or she will be perceived, especially in the professional world. *Everyone.* If that's true for you, take a deep breath and read on. Help is here.

When I meet with career coaching clients, we eventually talk about the documents that represent them in the professional world—resume, social media profiles, cover letter(s), and bio, if needed. At the beginning of our work together, I rarely see a resume that represents the good story of my client. The document I see usually shows a "just the facts" retelling of work history and some related information about tasks the individual has completed in past positions. Or, conversely, I see a document that retells every single point of the person's career history. This document is difficult to read because a reader can't identify what is essential to this person's story. If you fall into one of these categories, don't worry. Read on and you will find the answers to these challenges.

Everyone, including you, has a good story to tell. It's what makes you unique. Now, you might be thinking, "Great. Now I have to be unique." Don't worry, you've already got that covered. Just by being here in the world and having the experiences you've had, you are already unique. No one has lived the same life as you. *Voilà!* Uniqueness.

Let's approach your resume from an atypical angle. Let's think of it as a vehicle to convey your good story—as a collection of all your best working moments, the moments you are most proud of having experienced. Think of your resume as an artistic composition where you fit together the story of your professional past, what you are currently accomplishing, some conveyance of where you are headed, and what you will contribute to your new company.

I approach each resume as an interesting composition where the details of someone's professional life must be told in a compelling, easy-to-read format. It's a challenge and game to get each client's good story on the page. The following chapters will give you a step-by-step guide to creating a document that will convey your accomplishments while serving as a tool for organizing and sharing your professional progression. Given that you've picked up this book, chances are you are eager to get started developing the best resume you possibly can. You might have written a resume for yourself before; you might be new to resume writing because you are graduating from a higher education program or returning to work after an absence. You might also have questions about what constitutes the "best" resume because it seems that almost everyone has an opinion about style and content. I know this because clients come to me confused and with a list of questions.

To get us off to a good start, Chapter 2 deals with principles of effectiveness for resumes as well as my response to frequently asked questions. A careful reading of this section will set the foundation for the following chapters that guide you to build your resume step by step. Chapters 3 to 9 each delve deep into one section or element of the resume, including Profile, Skills, Experience, and Education. In these chapters, you'll learn how to express and showcase your skills and experience, as well as how to leverage your professional affiliations and volunteer activities. Chapter 10 will help you pull everything together for a compelling story of your best assets and potential. If you are a recent graduate, you'll be especially interested in Chapter 11, which is a bonus chapter just for you. Chapter 12 shares tips for the job application process. Finally, Chapter 13 presents complete sample resumes so you can review good examples of resumes in a variety of industries.

Once you've worked through the chapters in this book, you may not love writing a resume as much as I do, but I can guarantee you will have the tools to make sure your good story will be well represented.

CHAPTER 2

IT'S NOT A PICASSO ... IT'S YOUR RESUME

When I think of artwork by Picasso, I think of noses where ears should be and ears where mouths should be. I think of fragmented pieces that make a whole, where you really have to use your imagination to see the bigger picture. Resumes are not works by Picasso. A reader of your resume should be able to see the cohesive "story" in a matter of seconds. Although hiring managers and recruiters don't agree on a definitive number, all agree that they take *an average of 6 to 10 seconds* to scan your resume and determine if you'll be moving to the next step in their process.

Years ago, when I graduated from college, everyone was taught to write using a *reverse chronological* format. Your resume started with your contact information and then launched right into your work history, from most recent to least recent. Thankfully, that style is out of date.

For the last eight to ten years the *hybrid* style has been popular. The feature I like most about the hybrid style is that it encourages you to tell a bit of "story" in a Profile section at the top of the resume and also allows you to feature your best skills related to the prospective job, all before you start addressing work history. Don't you think that's a better way to start your resume?

These days, a resume is used to convey three pieces of information about you:

1. Who you are in the working world
2. What knowledge and skills you've accumulated
3. How you have used your knowledge and skills to benefit employers

What are the best elements to convey this information in a resume? I recommend using a format that includes the following four to five sections:

Profile
A profile outlines who you are and what traits you bring to the workplace, regardless of industry. It is a four-to-five statement section describing what characteristics you are best known for in the working world.

Skills

The Skills section tells the reader what you know. This is the place where you want to align what you know with the skills that are listed in a job posting. Keywords, which I explain in Chapter 4, are critical to determining whether your resume will be read or not. This is because many organizations use computer screening to sort resumes before they ever reach a person. If your resume doesn't contain the desired keywords, it will be rejected, even if you are highly qualified for the job in question.

Experience

The Experience section is where the broad brushstrokes of your description of yourself in the two previous sections is detailed more thoroughly. I call it, "where the rubber hits the road." The Experience section includes bullets of specific, quantifiable details about how you have contributed at your positions.

Education

The most straightforward section, the Education section, conveys your degrees, professional development, and other training.

Volunteer and Community Involvement

If applicable, a Volunteer and Community Involvement section can be added to the end of your resume to show your engagement in the greater community in which you live, and also to feature any leadership positions you have held outside of work; for example, you might indicate that you served as a coach for a team or as a board member for a nonprofit or professional organization.

You will notice I did not mention using an Objective Statement on your resume. An Objective Statement was used in the past to indicate what you were hoping to get out of a position or your career. Here's an example: *To obtain a position in which I can utilize my skills in resume development and career coaching while decreasing the hiring time for XYZ company.* Objective statements are outdated. Potential employers are most interested in how you can contribute to their organization—not the short-term or long-term goals you have for your career. Make sure that is the information you want to share on your resume. Good employers are also interested in your growth, but save talking about those goals for your interview.

The following chapters will coach you through creating a hybrid resume. Before you get started, I would like to share a few more essential resume pointers:

PRINCIPLES OF EFFECTIVENESS

Readability Is the #1 Most Important Design Element

Good design counts; organization is key. A poorly organized resume will get passed over in a matter of seconds. Literally. What makes readability? Continue reading …

Put the Most Important Information Where It Will Be Read

The job site, Ladders, sponsored a heat map eye study of where hiring managers and recruiters' eyes focus when reading a resume. A heat map eye study uses technology to track eye movements to determine the focus of viewers; in other words, it tracks what content is of the most and least interest.

The Ladders study found that most hiring managers and recruiters spend time scanning your name, most recent position titles, where you've worked, dates there, and achievements. In most cases, they don't read paragraphs of information (because those areas are too long to follow all the details). An effective resume uses bulleted or bolded information to draw the reader's eyes to information the writer wants to feature.

Pay Attention to Flow

The flow from one section of your resume to another matters to readers. That flow contributes to the readability I mentioned above. Think of your resume as a funnel of information, with the widest part at the top of your document. The first section, or Profile, describes *who you are*, the broadest brush strokes on your composition. The second section, the Skills or Qualifications section, describes *what you know*, adding some detail to your composition but not conveying the full picture. The next section, or Professional Experience, describes *how you do (did) it*. This is where the specifics of color and shading and enhancement all come together.

Organize your information from less specific to more specific, from more general information about your traits and attributes, to what specific information you know and skills you have, to how you combined those traits and skills to succeed on specific projects. Think of flow in a graphical sense, with the widest, most general part of your story at the top and the important details becoming more specific as the composition progresses:

WHO YOU ARE
(Profile)

WHAT YOU KNOW
(Skills or Qualifications)

HOW YOU DID IT
(Professional Experience)

Use Your Best Space for Your Best Information

Your most critical information—your story and skills—belongs on the top one-half to two-thirds of the first page of your resume. Think about how you read a magazine or newspaper, even a website—the information at the top of the page gets your attention. The same is true for your resume. Don't waste that valuable space on an Objective Statement, which is outdated, or your education details, which are usually just a check-off box for hiring managers.

Understand the Difference between Impact and Contribution and Describe Both

The most significant thing you can convey on your resume is the positive impact you have made at the organization(s) where you have worked. Contributions are often confused with impact. Contributions are the ways you participated or provided value to the projects or work of your company. Impact reflects the positive change you made at an organization.

In a perfect world, you will show both contributions and impact on your resume. However, impact is generally more important to hiring managers; they will use your impact to forecast your performance in future roles.

Because of this, you will want to know how the company or department measures impact. Examples include increasing net profit, market share, or efficiency. Find out what you can about how the company or department measures success and include your experience with those impacts on your resume.

Make Sure You, and the Way You Describe Yourself, Demonstrate the Right Fit

Kristin Flink Kranias, writer for online career support site The Muse (hosted by The Daily Muse, www.themuse.com), asked the most prolific hiring professionals the following question: "What is the most critical thing for candidates to convey to land the job?" Those professionals offered many different pieces of advice, but one issue emerged as a common thread—"fit."

What does that mean? Flink Kranias offers this definition:

> *Fit is about having a unique perspective that enhances the team while also proving you'll get along with the team.*

You convey fit through a resume by doing research on the company. Search local trade and news resources to learn about the company's priorities, current projects, and culture. Don't change who you are; instead, find companies and organizations that match your values and attributes and "speak their language" through your resume.

Frequently Asked Questions

I bet you're ready to start writing! To help you start, here are some answers to common questions:

One Page or Two?

Two pages in length is now standard. In 2018, the resume writing service, ResumeGo, presented almost 20,000 resumes to 482 recruiters, hiring managers, and human resources professionals. Across the group, a two-page resume was preferred over a one-page version.

One page makes you look too thin, and not in a good way. The most informative part of the ResumeGo experiment was that it found hiring professionals spend, on average, twice as long reviewing a resume when it is two pages instead of one page.

In some cases, it might be appropriate to have a one-page resume—a recent college graduate, for example. But, generally, you will want to use up to two pages to tell your story. There is even a recent trend that, if you have a lengthy and accomplished career progression, your resume can flow onto a third page, but think carefully before you do this. If you choose to go in this direction, do not use the entire third page. That would be considered too lengthy for a resume.

How Many Years of My Work History Should I Include?

Hiring managers generally like to see your past 10 to 15 years of work history. If you have a longer career and positions of note further back in your history, you can comfortably represent 20 years of experience. If you have relevant experience more than 20 years ago, you can use the phrasing, "Additional foundational experience … " with limited details and no dates. That tells the reader you have additional experience important to your professional progression, but that not all the details are important. See the sample Hybrid Resume – Alternative Executive Format in Chapter 13 for an example on how this looks on the page.

References or Not?

Putting references on your resume or including the "References available on request" statement at the bottom is outdated. If you are asked to supply your references with your resume, create a separate page, copying and pasting your header from your resume onto a new page, so your documents look coordinated.

What Font Should I Use?

There are so many choices of font to use on your resume. I prefer Helvetica for resumes with a more contemporary design since it is very easy to read and is not used as often as Arial. I like Book Antiqua, instead of Times New Roman, for more traditional resume designs since much of our printed material uses Times New Roman as the font and a reader's eyes can get "lazy" in picking up details. If you can't decide between a traditional or contemporary font, I find Optima to be a good compromise. You want to strike a balance between using a font different from what readers are used to seeing, but not so different that it is distracting.

There are three important factors to consider when choosing a font for your resume:

- Meet the reader where he or she is comfortable, meaning use a traditional font and layout if utilizing your resume in a more traditional field, like law, and use a more contemporary font and layout if utilizing your resume in a more progressive field, like tech.

- Choose a font that has interest to it and has not been overused in other printed material. You will stand out from the "crowd" of resumes if you present your material in a design that looks different from others but appealing.

- Lastly, save your resume in PDF version once it is completed since only a PDF will preserve your font choice across different computer platforms.

To Bold or Not to Bold?

Bolding certain areas—words, phrases, or statements—of your resume is the best way you can guide the reader through your resume. Use bolding strategically and purposefully.

To Italicize or Not to Italicize?

Unlike bolding, italicized text on your resume is very difficult to read in most fonts. Use italics sparingly.

Do I Have to Include My Street Address in My Header?

The header generally offers the hiring manager the best information by which to contact you. Always include an email address and one phone number. Including your address is optional. In some circumstances it will be beneficial; for example, if you are seeking a position where it's important that you live where you work, such as applying to a local nonprofit. It will be important to the organization that you know the community you will be serving. In other cases, you will want to minimize the location where you live; for example, if you are seeking work out of the region.

Branding Statement or Not?

These days, there is a lot of talk about "branding" in the working world. Branding statements are identifiers you can use in between the header of your resume (that includes your name and contact information) and your Profile section. Bill Chiaravalle, in Branding for Dummies, sums it up nicely, so I will borrow his definition: A branding statement is "a concise statement that defines what you do … and what you pledge to consistently deliver." A sample branding statement is "Marketing and Communications Professional/Specializing in Public Relations and Media."

There are pros and cons to using a branding statement. On the pro side, it helps your reader understand who you are and what you can do in just a few words. On the con side, it can be limiting if you choose descriptive words that don't say enough about what you can do. Ultimately, a branding statement helps readers to better understand what you're "selling." I suggest using one, but choosing your words wisely.

Whose Advice Should I Follow About Differing Formats, Etc.?

To maintain your sanity during the job seeking process, follow your instinct—or gut—and use a format for your resume and job seeking that resonates with you. Everyone, and I mean nine out of ten people you ask, will have an opinion. Follow that which feels right. The information in this workbook has been developed from writings, feedback, and conversations with hiring managers, human resource professionals, recruiters, decision makers, and my own years of experience. It is not comprehensive by any standard, but it is comprised of "best practice" information. Your family members and others might be well-meaning, but follow your instincts and the professionals you trust; ignore the other chatter.

QUICK GRAMMAR TIP

USE STATEMENTS, NOT SENTENCES, ON YOUR RESUME

Use a statement such as, "Highly focused, adaptable brand management professional experienced in all aspects of marketing consumer products in diverse environments" versus "I am a highly focused and adaptable brand management professional experienced in all aspects of marketing consumer products in diverse environments."

A sentence contains a subject ("I," in this case), verb ("experienced") and predicate ("brand management professional"). Starting with the more important descriptive words—"highly focused, adaptable"—creates more interest for the reader. Note that by removing the subject, you no longer have sentences; therefore, you do not need periods at the ends of your statements. So, use statements, not sentences, and skip the periods on your resume. Trust me, it will be a more compelling read.

TRUISM

Think of your resume not only as a tool for prospective employers; think of it as a way to hold and curate your professional story. The more regularly you add to or update your resume, the easier it will be to have it ready to submit when an opportunity arises.

YOUR PROFILE IS A SELF-PORTRAIT PAINTED BY YOUR MOST CRITICAL JUDGE—YOU!

As we were getting to know each other at an introductory appointment, Julie passed her resume across the table. On it she referred to herself as a "multi-tasker" and "team player," able to "successfully complete the sales process" while "able to meet the goals of the company."

Knowing Julie had been working as a Regional Territory Manager in sales and was seeking a Vice President role, I asked why she had used such generic descriptors for herself and her skills. Her reply was one I hear often, "I don't know what else to say about myself."

I pointed out that the Profile section on Julie's resume would be the first thing read by a hiring manager. She could use that space to list attributes that make her special, uniquely valuable to future employers, as well as the many reasons why she should be hired. Wouldn't it be more interesting to focus on what makes her unique rather than using words everyone else would have on his or her resume? Yes!

For example, if Julie's Profile section looks like this, it has the capacity to leave the reader wanting to know more about her, which is a good thing:

> Positive, high-energy business development leader with deep and diverse industry experience in Media and Advertising, including Print, Digital Marketing, Radio, TV, Cable, and e-Commerce technologies ♦ Visionary thought leader who capably solves problems methodically from development through execution and control ♦ Cultivates strategy and is driven by efficient, analytical decision-making utilizing qualitative and quantitative data ♦ Collaborative and active listener who successfully builds strong relationships across all areas of the company and the industry

Since the Profile section is the first area to define the professional *you* in descriptive terms, use it to share information about where you want to go. What do you want your new "brand" to be? Julie was a Regional Territory Manager, but she aspired to move into a Vice President role. Having her Profile focused more on her vision and strategy traits—"big picture" thinking—makes her more desirable in that role.

Remember the information funnel from Chapter 2? The Profile section is where you will start to use it to guide your writing, getting to tell your unique story of *who you are*, *what you're known for*, and *what—attributes or character traits—you bring to the table in professional situations*.

TIPS ON DRAFTING A GREAT PROFILE

Create Your Profile with Four to Five Statements about Yourself

Think about times when you have been happiest in your work, past or present. On a piece of paper, jot down the traits you most enjoyed sharing through your work during those times. For example, Julie's second bullet, "*Visionary thought leader who capably solves problems methodically from development through execution and control*" came from such an exercise. She remembered a time when she had a role in a company that allowed her more autonomy and she was able to exercise creative vision and project management capabilities to solve problems.

Your First Statement Gets the Most Attention

The first statement in your Profile section is the one that will get the most attention. It should serve as the overview of who you are and where you have been. Think of this first statement as an "elevator pitch" or networking blurb about yourself. The goal is to make it descriptive enough that, if the hiring manager reads nothing else in the Profile section, he or she will have enough information about you to start to understand you and how you've been spending your time professionally. Here is the formula I use:

Adjective (or adjectives), noun "with deep experience" (or "with diverse experience"), what, where

For example, my client Carrie, a sales professional, wanted to move into a higher level business development role but needed to summarize her past success in sales roles. We decided to use the following as an opening statement for Carrie:

Goal-driven, loyal (adjectives) sales management leader (noun) with award-winning performance in program development and sales direction, along with technical-clinical experience (what) in the medical device industry (where)

Tells more of a story, right?

The Next Bullets Highlight Your Best Attributes

Then, for the next three to four bullets, highlight your best attributes. The formula I use for those bullets is:

Adjective or adverb, verb, details

Continuing with Carrie's resume, her next bullet states:

> Capably (adverb) listens (verb) to customer needs, asks probing questions, and creates customized selling techniques utilizing consultative selling process and Sandler Training (details)

As you can see, this statement offers much more detail and differentiation of the candidate than, "Capably completes the selling process, delivering company goals."

The Story Behind a Particular Word

When crafting the bullets, try to think of more of the story behind a particular word to describe yourself. How do you think you are different from others? Make sure to differentiate yourself. Your words count! This is how Carrie's complete Profile ended up:

> Goal-driven, loyal sales management leader with award-winning performance in program development and sales direction in the medical device industry ♦ Capably listens to customer needs, asks probing questions, and creates customized selling techniques utilizing consultative selling process and Sandler Training ♦ Drives the sales process by initiating collaborative team management which helps team members create customer buy-in, initiating forward action ♦ Highly accountable to teams, organizational heads, and stakeholders; comfortably communicates across the selling continuum

PRINCIPLES OF EFFECTIVENESS FOR YOUR PROFILE SECTION

Use Bulleted Statements Instead of Sentences in a Paragraph

Resume readers tend to ignore most information presented in paragraph format, which is why I prefer to list things in bulleted statements. Even if the statements are in paragraph format, I include bullets between statements because the bullet gives the eye a "resting" place. See the difference in the samples below:

Without bullets:

> Collaborative, community-focused non-profit leader with deep experience in multi-cultural, community, non-profit settings. Recognized for outstanding skills in connecting with the right people and organizations to achieve program goals. Enjoys working with and mentoring others to build capacity for organizations. Effective advocate who connects community needs with available local, state, and national resources

With bullets:

> Collaborative, community-focused non-profit leader with deep experience in multi-cultural, community, non-profit settings ♦ Recognized for outstanding skills in connecting with the best people and organizations to achieve program goals ♦ Enjoys working with and mentoring others to build capacity for organizations ♦ Effective advocate who connects community needs with available local, state, and national resources

Choose Your First and Last Statements Carefully

As a culture, we have relatively short attention spans. When you order your bullets, follow the rule of primacy and recency (otherwise known as the *serial position effect*), which states:

> *When given a list of information and later asked to recall that information, the items at the beginning (**primacy**) and the items at the end (**recency**) are more likely to be recalled than the items in the middle.*

Follow this guideline in any bulleted section of your resume. List your most significant bullet first, place the lesser information in the middle of the section, and end with another strong bullet. A former client, Jeanine, had a wonderful way of summarizing this ordering as "best, good, mediocre, mediocre, and good." I have been using that way of summarizing the serial position effect ever since!

Know Which Words Have the Highest Impact

Two phrases that have the potential to catch the eye of the reader and present a more compelling story of you are "recognized as" and "known for." These phrases are especially powerful on your resume because they imply that someone else is saying these things about you rather than you saying them about yourself. Using the Profile statement above as an example,

Without the "recognized for" statement

   Outstanding skills in connecting with the right people and organizations to achieve program goals

With the "recognized for" statement

   Recognized for outstanding skills in connecting with the right people and organizations to achieve program goals

The "recognized for" statement gives that bullet (and candidate) a little bit more oomph.

Use Descriptive Words That Have More Impact

The following are sample words you can use to describe your nouns and verbs:

Accomplished at	Adaptable	Adept	Adeptly	Approachable
Capable	Capably	Collaborative	Decisive	Diligent
Energetic	Expert at	Expertly	Highly	Inspiring
Positive	Practical	Proficient in	Recognized for	Relatable
Respected	Thorough	Thoughtful	Visionary	Well-versed at

Each year, several web-based resources publish a list of the 10 most overused words in resumes and on LinkedIn profiles. Most years, "innovative," "problem solver," "strategic," and "multi-tasker" are on those lists. Given the wealth of online resources to use, no excuses exist for not being able to find the right words. My favorite is Dictionary.com, which can be downloaded as an app to your smartphone or accessed through a web browser. Dictionary.com has an excellent thesaurus function, offering many substitutes for favorite words so you don't need to use the same words repeatedly.

QUICK TIP

WHAT TO CAPITALIZE

I am often asked questions about what words to capitalize and what words not to capitalize on resumes. Follow this rule: Any word that is a section header (ex. Profile, Skills, etc.), company or position name (ex. Development Director), title of a department (ex. Outside Sales) or name for a program (ex. Sandler Sales Training) should be capitalized. Other words that are not the "official" title of something (ex. sales department) can remain in lower case letters.

TRUISM

If it's boring for you to read, it will be boring to others. Dig deep to come up with meaningful phrases about yourself. Ask friends, family, and coworkers to read your resume and see how interesting it is for each to read. Add details, as necessary, to engage readers.

NOW YOU TRY IT

Consider the following questions:

What are the five to seven traits you bring to a workplace regardless of industry?

What are you known for?

If I asked your coworkers to describe you, what traits would they list?

1. _____

2. _____

3. _____

4. _____

5. _____

Next, expand those words into phrases that describe how you utilize those traits (you can combine words or use more than one in a phrase). For example, if you identified "thorough" and "responsive," your bullet could state, "Recognized for being highly responsive to customer needs, delivering thorough results that meet goals."

Expand on each of the traits listed above to create unique bullets:

1. _____

2. _____

3. _____

4. _____

5. _____

Also, create a bullet in the first position (remember primacy and recency?) that starts with some nice descriptive words about you, answers who you are professionally (title), what kind of experience you have, in what industry(ies). For example, "Committed, inspiring Customer Support Manager with experience leading teams in providing excellent customer service in manufacturing and retail environments."

Who you are: _____

Your experience: _____

Where/In what industry(ies): _____

Lastly, after the first bullet above (the most important bullet), decide how your bullets will be ordered in your Profile section based on the "best, good, mediocre, mediocre, good" guideline.

Best, for example"

Committed, inspiring Customer Support Manager with experience leading teams in providing excellent customer service in manufacturing and retail environments

Your Best: _____

Good: _____

Mediocre: _____

Mediocre: _____

Good: _____

CHAPTER 4

IT'S ALL ABOUT THE COLORS—MAKING YOUR SKILLS SHINE

Can you imagine a favorite work of art, Monet's "Water Lilies," for example, as shades of black, white, and gray? It loses some (all?) of its impact. It's about the colors! The colors are what take your breath away when you walk into the room with "Water Lilies." Like a great work of art, the details in the Skills section of your resume will add depth, dimension, and interest to your resume.

The previous chapter focused on "who you are." Now it is time to share "what you know." The purpose of this section is to describe the skills you bring to your next job. This section can be organized under many different titles, including Skills, Summary of Skills, Summary of Qualifications, Qualifications and Skills, Qualifications, Core Competencies, etc.

I like to pick a name for this section that matches your audience or reader. For example, if you are utilizing your resume in a traditional environment, such as banking or law, you might want to use the more formal header of Summary of Qualifications and Skills. If you are seeking a position in a trendier environment, such as a cutting-edge PR agency, you can use the less formal, Skills header. If you have had years of leadership and are at the C-level of any organization, consider using the header, Organizational Expertise and Leadership. Professionals in technology tend to use the Core Competencies header. You can research what your desired industry uses by looking online at sample resume templates in that field. The point is to know your reader and know what level of formality is appropriate for your resume.

Regularly, I read client resumes or see sample hybrid resumes on websites that include a nice, well-rounded profile, but the skills are listed without detail. Here is a list from a resume of someone seeking a senior position in HR. Does this list look familiar to you?

Executive Team Leadership	P/L Management
Negotiation	Process Improvement
Staff Training	Change Management

A list of skills with no other details is ineffective for two main reasons: not enough differentiation and lack of keywords.

A list offers no differentiation between you and the next person with the same or similar list. You lose the opportunity to really shine by telling more of the story of your range of experience. Sure, you know how to train staff, but you can also say, "adept at all aspects of HR, including recruiting, hiring, training, reviewing, and disciplining staff."

Effective resumes target keywords, something a generic list can't do. Keywords are the important words that are in job postings and the words entered into online application systems to "weed out" candidates who apply. The higher the keyword match, the more likely you are to get advanced onto the next phase in the application or interview process. Keywords are so important that you will have a hard time finding an article, blog post, or any other career-related information that doesn't mention them.

Keywords help to convey to the reader (or online system) that you speak the language of the posted position and company. Using longer, more descriptive bullets in your Skills section allows you to embed more keywords into your resume. For example, here is a posting, with keywords highlighted:

XYZ COMPANY SEEKS A SENIOR HR BUSINESS PARTNER

The Senior HR Business Partner is both a strategic and hands-on role that provides full cycle HR support to our initiatives around flexible fulfillment centers. The role is critical in executing our people initiatives, providing great internal customer support, and driving HR functional excellence and process improvement.

Successful candidates will demonstrate the following:

- ✓ The ability to understand business goals and recommend new approaches, policies, and procedures to effect continual improvements in business objectives, productivity, and development of HR within the company

- ✓ A true hands-on approach as well as the ability to successfully monitor the "pulse" of the employees to ensure a high level of employee engagement

- ✓ Passion for innovative HR solutions and process improvement; demonstrated experience driving process improvements, and specific skills in Kaizen methodologies preferred

- ✓ Strong project management skills; ability to lead projects at a network level to influence and obtain buy-in, and then drive execution and achievement of the right results

✓ Success in creating and driving effective employee relations, retention, and reward programs

✓ The ability to be comfortable with high-volume workload and not be afraid to "roll up your sleeves"

✓ A strong solutions focus and comfortable working in an environment which demands strong deliverables along with the ability to identify problems and drive appropriate solutions

✓ Strong internal and external customer service focus

✓ Excellent organizational and interpersonal skills

Here are sample bullets written to match the keywords in this posting:

- **Employee Retention and Relations** – skilled at building unique employee engagement and reward programs that increase retention/decrease turnover; leverages strong interpersonal skills that encourage positive employee relations, reducing safety risks and employee disciplinary action

- **Project Management** – certified Project Management Professional (PMP) and Lean Six Sigma Green Belt; knowledgeable in utilizing Kaizen methodologies; capably identifies problems, appropriate solutions, and gains buy-in at each point in the project life cycle, resulting in strong deliverables and goal achievement

- **Customer Service** – strong ability to identify problems and work toward appropriate "win-win" solutions; "preaches" a customer-first mentality with team, encouraging strong internal and external customer service; executes with advanced interpersonal skills

- **Process Improvement** – excels at creating cutting-edge, novel approaches to solve company HR challenges; effectively crafts policies and procedures that are "best practices" within industry

---

QUICK TIP
SAVE THE LAST BULLET (5TH OR 6TH) FOR LISTING YOUR TECHNICAL SKILLS

For example:
Technical Skills – knowledge of Windows software including Microsoft Word, Outlook, Excel, PowerPoint; Adobe, Digital Documents, Salesforce; skillful at Internet; experienced in database management, reports, and calendaring systems

---

A skills list can give the reader a general idea of your knowledge, but including details after the listed skill helps the reader understand your range of knowledge in a given area. In short, they demonstrate a match. The more detailed skills you have, the more desirable you will be to a prospective employer and the more likely your resume is to be picked out of the applicant pile.

Because it's important to create a resume that "speaks" to each posting or opportunity, use the Skills section of your resume to customize for each position to which you apply. If you are applying to similar positions in a single industry or field, create a separate document with 10-12 skills bullets. Use this document to swap skills bullets in and out of your resume to mirror those listed in the postings as you apply for different positions. If you are applying to positions in different industries, create a separate document with bullets for each unique industry.

Here is the formula that I suggest using when creating your bullets:

Overarching skill (bolded) – details of "story" after; the details of what you know/areas of experience

For example:

- **Research and Data** – applies specialized research skills (story), including market and trend research, survey development, data collection, measurement, and analysis (detail)

QUICK TIP

A WORD ABOUT LENGTH OF BULLETS

Hiring managers read (skim, really) your resume for appropriateness to position. There is a delicate balance between having enough and too much information. When talking to clients about length of bullets, I advise them to consider writing two to three lines of good, descriptive text in the Skills section, and not more. You want to avoid the phenomena of "reader fatigue." Fatigue is defined as "a subjective feeling of tiredness that has a gradual onset." A reader—your resume reader—can get this kind of fatigue when reading sections of your resume. To avoid this, include rich information and good details within your bullets. Again, if you are bored reading it, a hiring manager will be too.

TRUISM

Your uniqueness will make the difference! The more of a story you can tell about your knowledge base, the more unique and desirable you will be as a candidate.

NOW YOU TRY IT

Consider the following questions: What are the five to seven broad skill areas or bodies of knowledge you have related to your field?

For example:

"Team Recruitment and Training" or "Customer Service."

1. _____

2. _____

3. _____

4. _____

5. _____

6. _____

7. _____

Next, think of some of the details related to that skill.

For example:

"capably recruits, vets, and onboards team members; adept at creating online, video, and written training materials."

1. _____

2. _____

3. _____

4. _____

5. _____

Merge the information to create cohesive bullets.

For example:

Team Recruitment and Training – capably recruits, vets, and onboards team members; adept at creating online, video, and written training materials

1. _____ – _____

   _____

2. _____ – _____

   _____

3. _____ – _____

   _____

4. _____ – _____

   _____

5. _____ – _____

   _____

Finally, decide how your bullets will be ordered in your Skills section based on the "best, good, mediocre, mediocre, good" guideline and what you think will be most important to the hiring manager reading your resume.

Most Important: _____

Important: _____

Less Important: _____

Less Important: _____

Important: _____

CHAPTER 5

It's All About the Shading—Getting the Details Right

The next step of resume creation is for you to share how you utilize(d) your traits and skills to contribute and make change within specific companies and organizations, otherwise known as the Experience section. The Experience section is where you will articulate how you utilized your traits from the Profile section and knowledge from the Skills section to excel in your former work environments, sharing information about your tasks, responsibilities, and select accomplishments.

Format First

Different types of career progression will require slightly different presentations in your Experience section. I work with clients from most industries and at every point in their career. Some have worked multiple positions at different companies; some have held multiple positions at the same company; some have held the same position for a number of years. For example, Steve has worked progressive positions in leadership and fundraising, moving to a different company every four to five years; Bob has worked at a medical supply firm for 20 years but has had four different positions within the company; Jennifer has worked at one manufacturing company for 18 years in a single position.

Here are guidelines to "tell" those stories in a readable, understandable format:

For Progressive Positions at Multiple Companies

List the company first, justified to the left side of your document. List dates worked at the company in a right column justified on the right side of your document. List the title of your position underneath the company name, and then list five to seven bullets underneath. Continue to use this format for each position.

Another example:

Greater Community Partnership   **2014 – present**
Director of Development

- Executes as primary fundraising and community networking professional for organization; develops collaborative projects and agency budgeting

- Next descriptive bullet

- Etc.

For Progressive Positions at a Single Company

List company first, justified to the left side of your document. List *total* dates worked at the company in a right column justified on the right side of your document, on the same line as the company name. List the title of your *most recent* position underneath the company name, indented five spaces. List dates worked *in that position* in parentheses after the title of that position and then list five to seven bullets underneath. When you move to listing the second most recent position, repeat the process of listing the title of your *most recent* position underneath, indented five spaces (no need to relist the company name), listing dates worked *in that position* in parentheses after the title of that position, and then listing five to seven bullets underneath.

For example:

Drugs-for-You Pharmaceutical Company   **2005 – present**
Region Sales Executive (2012 – present)

- Responsible for the clinical positioning and sale of company's operating room solutions to maintain and grow overall business over a $15M base of business

- Improved the profitability of the region by focusing on high-margin products and collaborating with account managers to identify margin-improvement opportunities and implement solutions and strategies

- Provides field mentoring, coaching, and training assistance to account managers through the region; team includes 12 account managers

- Effectively communicates and collaborates with multiple functional teams to develop new solutions by proactively recommending creative improvements to products, services, and process based on customer and user needs

Region Sales Manager (2009 – 2012)

- Managed 5 sales representatives and had complete responsibility for a $20M region covering Pennsylvania, Ohio, and Kentucky

- Consistently achieved sales goals through leadership in the development of strategies and objectives, as well as directing the development and implementation of tactical plans

Sales Representative (2005 – 2009)

- Managed and expanded large territory by 20% in medical/surgical disposables in a highly competitive market

- Represented vast product line, including surgical non-woven drapes and gowns, personal protective equipment, orthopedic soft goods, surgical and exam gloves, and a variety of patient care products

- Collaborated with medical distributors to sell medical supplies and services

For a Single Position Held for Most of Career at a Single Company

List company first, justified to the left side of your document. List dates worked at the company in a right column justified on the right side of your document. List the title of your position underneath the company name, then use subheaders identifying the different areas of your responsibilities to create bulleted lists of three, five, or seven detailed bullets underneath.

For example:

Director of Business Development   **1999 – present**
Greater Hamilton Convention & Visitors Bureau

Sales

- Started at organization as Sales Manager and was promoted to newly created position of Director of Business Development in October 2009

- Fosters business relationships and creates collaborative projects to enhance and refine a $7M organization and $1.37B industry

- Booked 5 new major events to organization in FY 2017

- Increased membership to organization 110+% to goal every year since 2009

Programming

- Directs and manages partnerships and programs contributing to efficiencies and growth in accordance with the targeted goals and objectives; increased program attendance by 35-50% in FYs 2015 – 2018

- Spearheaded pilot program for Hamilton City residents with associated incentives for utilizing services and programs

Outreach

- Responsible for administering grant program, community enhancement and outreach initiatives, as well as strengthening partner, customer, and supplier relationships

- Collaborates with department heads and President/CEO for implementation of special projects in community

- Acts as "face of the GHC&VB" at community events; engaged in multiple community organizations

Listing Dates

You'll notice differences in where I've placed the dates. When at one position at multiple companies, you need only list the dates you were at each company because they will provide continuity to the dates you held the position before. However, when listing multiple positions held at a single company, list *the total time you were at the company and the dates you held each position.*

Lastly, when listing dates at positions on your resume, utilize the numerical form, instead of writing out the months. For example, "2015 – present" or "1/2018 – 12/2018." In this format, they are easier to read. In general, only include months (1, 2, 3, 4, etc.) when you have been employed at a position for less than a year or if it will help to show greater longevity at a position; for example, "2/2017 – 10/2018" versus "2017 – 2018."

> QUICK TIP
>
> WHAT YOU WERE OR WHERE YOU WERE?
>
> Sometimes the title of the position you held at a company will be more important than the company itself. For example, it will be more important to the reader that you held the position of Chief Information Officer than the company that you worked for if that company is not very well-known. The opposite is true if you've held the same position (Accountant) at multiple high-profile companies (Cleveland Clinic, Eaton, and Sherwin-Williams). Choose if it's more important to emphasize *what you were* or *where you were*. Bold the information you determine is more important.

CONTENT STILL COUNTS IN THE DESCRIPTIVE BULLETS FOR EACH POSITION!

As I discussed in Chapter 2, readability and capturing your reader's interest is most important on your resume. The first tip is to start each of your bullets with a word that catches the reader's attention, usually a verb (using present or past tense as appropriate).

Here is a list of some commonly used verbs:

Facilitates	Provides	Leads	Developed
Manages	Directs	Oversees	Created
Contributes	Increases	Designs	Mentors

Here is a list of some of my favorite "pumped up" verbs:

Encourages	Engages	Positions
Transformed	Moved	Elevated (love this one!)

After leading with a strong action verb, the rest of your bullet can describe the *who, what,* and *how* in relation to you performing this activity. Everyone wants to read something that catches their attention; no one wants to read a "just the facts" listing of your responsibilities in a position. Instead, include interesting tidbits about your responsibilities.

For example:

Okay

> Interacted with board to encourage greater participation in the grant-making process

Better

> Increased board member participation in grant-making from one member in 2015 to over 20, comprising 45% of all funding review team members by 2018

Which person would you contact for the interview if you were hiring? The details that help make this bullet especially interesting are the numbers—the quantification of impact you made. Specific information makes that bullet more engaging to read. Again, remember that the information will differentiate you from other candidates who might have similar characteristics on paper.

Below are more examples of how to "amp up" your bulleted information in your experience:

Okay

> Directed the reporting and centralized company financial data onto new software

Better

> Redesigned all reporting for company-wide consistency; centralized all financial data; updated technology, migrating from 10-year-old system to state-of-the-art software; and instituted strong bank-wide financial procedures

Okay

> Collaborated with several downtown companies on charitable giving that increased visibility and reputation of company

Better

> Built partnerships with 7 corporations in downtown Cleveland office complex for the purpose of combined charity and fundraising drives; collaboration raised $120K in the first year and brought in new business from 3 majors accounts

Okay

> Hired and trained over 200 employees who achieved promotions; developed 15 assistant managers, increasing effectiveness of organization

Better

> Hired, trained, coached, and led over 200 employees earning promotions into key positions throughout the organization; coached and developed 15 assistant managers which resulted in earning a promotion to manager within 9 months and created future leaders throughout the organization

EVIDENCE OF IMPACT

I often talk about "impact" as describing outcomes rather than activities. What did you accomplish and how did you make change at the organizations or companies where you worked? Hiring managers state the most important information to read about any candidate are accomplishments and evidence of change-making at an organization. Include information that you can quantify, and show improvement in monetary gain/savings or process improvement.

For example:

Recognized as Top Producer for achieving $18M in new product sales within 8 months of employment

or

Opened first-time territories in Chicago and Dallas through prospecting and account development; built a base of business to provide sustained revenue, enabling the company to open local sales offices in each market

Include good information in the bullets that describe your experience, but also feature these special game changers at the end of your bulleted sections. You can do this after each position or in a separate section. Chapter 6 provides a complete description of how to feature these game changers.

SPECIAL CIRCUMSTANCES:
THIS IS FOR YOU, STAY-AT-HOME MOMS AND
OTHERS WHO THINK YOU HAVE NO EXPERIENCE

Joanne came to me wanting to get back into the working world after 15 years of staying home and raising children. She was in despair both because she didn't think she had been "doing anything" work-related for the past 15 years and because she had no idea what to put on paper for those years. As we discussed her goals and interests, Joanne mentioned that she had been president of her children's Parent-Teacher Organization for five years. Then she told me she had been fundraising chair for an organization for three separate events—and raised over $25,000 each time. Lastly, Joanne talked about being part of the membership recruitment team for her community's high school band boosters. She was responsible for finding and recruiting other parents and orienting new members to the group. The skills involved in these tasks are transferable to many workplaces.

Joanne's next concern was that she would have to leave behind this type of work in order to contribute financially to her family. Not so! I immediately thought that nonprofit fundraising work would be an ideal fit, and that with all the experience listed above, she had much to "talk" about on her resume. But, how to talk about it?

In Joanne's case and in other circumstances where your unpaid or volunteer experiences provide excellent examples of your skills and working "stories," I recommend titling the Experience section Related Experience instead of Professional Experience. "Professional" implies that you were paid for the work that you did, but Related Experience can include paid and unpaid work, rather than listing the details in a later Volunteer Experience section that may or may not get read at the end of your resume. See the following example of how to list this type of experience:

RELATED EXPERIENCE
Membership Chair   **2016 – present**
Hamilton High School Band Boosters

- Oversees and coordinates recruitment efforts for 200 member support organization; increased membership 25% in first year

- Provides orientation to new members, which includes explaining committee options and purpose of each, pairing each new member with a mentor, and serving as the point person for any questions

- Attends other high school events as a representative of the group, sharing information on purpose and involvement

I recommend using the Related Experience header in any circumstance where you have unpaid work (an internship, volunteer work, etc.) that supports your professional brand and what you are pursuing for future work.

A WORD ABOUT HOW WE TALK ABOUT OURSELVES: A MARS/VENUS MOMENT

Some of the differences between how work—or the words you use to describe your work—are evaluated based on gender and, as a result, how resumes are viewed. In 2018, *Harvard Business Review* reported on a study, conducted by Hebl, Nittrouer Corrington, and Madera, in which the language of hundreds of resumes, produced by male and female applicants, was compared.

Across the study, women tended to use *communal* words, such as "caring," "kind," and "collegial." Men used more *agentic* words—which were interpreted to indicate that men are psychologically perceived as producers. Agentic words include "determined," "dedicated," and "charismatic." Most important, the study found reader bias regarding the applicants, regardless of whether the position applied for was more traditionally female (nursing, for example) or male (paramedic, for example). Communal words were always viewed as less desirable traits than agentic words.

Another 2018 study, conducted by Linda Babcock, Maria P. Recalde, and Lise Vesterlund, revealed that women are far more likely to engage in "non-promotable tasks" than men at work. Additionally, men are more comfortable saying no to tasks or projects that they deem as less important, or likely to be viewed as unimportant, and women are more likely to volunteer when others will not. That can also translate to how information is read on your resume. Were the projects you engaged in important to the company or organization? Were you a difference-maker? Here are some things to think about as you prepare to write your bullets for your Experience section:

- Use your descriptive language carefully, understanding that words can mean different things to different people.

- Determine which tasks and projects were viewed as important to the past and current organizations and feature those, providing some explanation as to why they were important.

- Now and in the future, volunteer for more of what you determine are more promotable tasks and keep track of your engagement, especially the result or outcome of those projects.

In her book *Accelerate Your Impact*, executive strategist and speaker on leadership issues, JJ DiGeronimo addresses the gap in details shared by men and women via their resumes. She references a study in which "91 percent of men include bulleted verb statements that describe their achievements, but only 36 percent of women do." The take-home message is that women need to do a better job articulating details of achievement on their resumes.

Unfortunately, people are judged on issues unrelated to their work history. This is especially true for women. Whatever your gender, make sure to include ample examples of past accomplishments and projects where you have contributed to the goals or bottom line of your company, especially in the Experience section. Also, be aware of the language you use to describe yourself. Think about how it will be interpreted. If you are a woman, pay special attention to the number of communal words you use and decide if you need to include more agentic words.

QUICK TIP
BREAK THE RULE FOR NUMBERS AND DOLLAR FIGURES

List numbers and dollar figures in numerical form, instead of written words, For example, *5 team members* instead of *five team members* and *$1M* instead of *$1 million dollars*. Those characters will "jump" off the page, drawing the reader's eye to important details. It is against the grammatical rule that states numbers ten and under are written out instead of presented in numerical format, but this is a place where you can break that rule.

FREQUENTLY ASKED QUESTIONS

What About Less Traditional Work Experience?

Stay-at-Home Parenting

Think comprehensively about your volunteer experience and other things you have done during your parenting time. What activities included work-related skills, such as bookkeeping, budgeting, organizing, or multiple task management? Include those activities and tasks on your resume as Related Experience.

College Students or Graduating Students

Graduating from any higher education program, whether it be with a bachelor's degree or an associate's degree, often represents a challenge in creating a resume since you might think you don't have enough "real" work experience. Not true!

You might not have what I call one-to-one experience, where you have held a similar job before, but you do have relevant experience. It is all about how you depict and organize the experience you have, as well as communicating the *potential* you have to offer. Feel free to skip to Chapter 11 in which I have outlined my recommendations for this circumstance.

From Independent Business Owner to Team Member of a Larger Company

You will be in a position of rebranding yourself from one career to another and communicating your value in the new position or industry. Take time to write a list of all the skills you have related to your first career and how each can relate to your second career. Refer to those skills in your Skills section.

You will want to rebrand yourself as a team player. Give special emphasis to any experience you have interacting with others—clients, vendors, salespeople, and other organizational representatives. Those skills "speak" to your ability to interact well with others. Most employers value your strengths in getting along well with others over knowing how to do all the technical aspects of the job.

TRUISM

Put yourself in the shoes of a prospective employer; what would you want to read on a resume? What would you like to know about someone like you? What skills would you like to see? Answer those questions.

ACTIVITY TO RECONNECT WITH YOUR SKILLS

We often forget, in our long or short career history (or even our day-to-day life), the skills we have or enjoy using. The activity below will help you identify the skills you brought to a particular job or task in your life.

If you have a limited career history, use any volunteer positions (*ex. Speaker Coordinator for community group—organized, good at establishing relationships, ability to see needs, etc.*) or daily roles (*ex. Primary Caregiver for my young child—diplomatic, patient, good at time management*). Once you have completed the list, identify with a star (*) those skills that you particularly enjoy using.

What Skills Do I Have?

Position: _____

Skill 1 _____

Skill 2 _____

Skill 3 _____

Skill 4 _____

Skill 5 _____

Position: _____

Skill 1 _____

Skill 2 _____

Skill 3 _____

Skill 4 _____

Skill 5 _____

Position: _____

Skill 1 _____

Skill 2 _____

Skill 3 _____

Skill 4 _____

Skill 5 _____

Once you have identified your positions and skills, merge them together into the format for "Related Experience."

For example:

Public Relations and Marketing Chair   **2016 – present**
Smithville High School Choir Coordinators
- Produces monthly newsletter with circulation to 200+ families
- Creates and coordinates circulation of all PR materials for Smithville High School Show Choir; materials include posters, flyers, and press releases
- Attends relevant local community events to promote choir activities

You will find you have more career-related experience than you thought you had!

Chapter 6

Additional Impact to Your Work of Art—Adding Embellishments

When Michelle began telling me about her professional accomplishments, she recounted a long list of awards and projects in which she had significantly contributed to change-making at her organization. The resume she showed me prior to our work together had those accomplishments hidden within her position bullets. They did not shine in the way they needed to.

Nearly everyone has had key projects he or she has worked on or, in many cases, awards or recognition for work well done. There are two ways you can present these exceptional accomplishments so they get the attention they deserve: 1) as a separate section; or 2) as special Key Accomplishment bullets at the end of each position.

As a Separate Section

There are several name choices for the separate section choice. It can be called Select Accomplishments if most of the bullets refer to achievements you have realized or for which you've been acknowledged. Some positions or industries are very award-driven. For example, positions in sales have multiple awards associated with them like "President's Club," "Top Achiever of the Year," and "Rising Star." In that case, it will best serve you to title this section Select Awards and Accomplishments. Other industries aren't as geared toward awards but are more interested in change-making projects. In that case, feature your best three or four projects that show your knowledge and initiative. Listing three to four of your best projects will add to your overall appeal as a candidate. I call these mini-stories "the icing on the cake." In that case, title this section Key Accomplishments or Key Projects.

If you choose to add the separate section, your resume will be ordered this way: Profile, Skills, Select Key Projects (or Select Awards and Accomplishments), Experience, etc. By placing these significant projects in a separate section, on the first page, hiring managers will see your most important work up front.

For example:

SELECT KEY PROJECTS AND AWARDS

Recognized as #1 salesperson within a team of 18; in the past three years, maintained a ranking in the top 5 (2017)

Creative Solution Selling Award, based on an innovative solution to a customer need (2016)

35% growth over prior year achieving increased net earnings from $20M to $27M (2015)

Beat launch timeline and maintained limited budget ($5M) for new product launch

Re-envisioned training materials, cutting training time by 20%

You may also choose to feature accomplishments as outlined below:

Listing Key Accomplishment(s) at the End of Each Position You've Listed in the "Experience Section"

In this format, each accomplishment will "live" with the position where you achieved that distinction but still be featured as an accomplishment. For example:

Tech Stars   **2013 – present**
Vice President

- Provides operational oversight for a $25M IT staffing firm

- Directs the development of tools and teams that will promote fiscal growth and stability as related to the business plan of creating the IT staffing segment as a revenue-enhancing segment of the overall staffing

- Led the effort to develop an Applicant Tracking System that ties to custom database, reducing position fill time by 25%

- Developed sales collateral for deployment within the first 90 days; initiated plan that landed 5 new high-yield accounts within 6 months

- Refined and expanded compensation plans for sales and recruiting staff

Key Accomplishments
- Launched an applicant tracking system that saved the company over 20K hours annually

QUICK TIP

CREATE GREATER INTEREST FOR THE READER

To draw even more attention to special sections on your resume, like those featuring accomplishments, you can change up the justification. For example, in the Select Key Projects and Awards section above, the text is centered on the page. By changing the format slightly, but not too dramatically or too often, you create greater interest for the reader.

CHAPTER 7

ADDITIONAL CHARACTERS IN YOUR COMPOSITION—INCLUDING PROFESSIONAL AFFILIATIONS

Steve, the fundraiser from Chapter 5, thought we were done talking about edits to his resume when we finished the Experience section, stating, "So, now I just include my education and I'm good to go!" Well, not necessarily, if you want it to be as complete as possible. Two more sections complete your professional composition.

During our discussions, Steve had referenced a number of groups he belonged to and events he attended, including the local Chamber of Commerce, the Association of Fundraising Professionals, and a local philanthropic organization for which he served as a board member. None of these activities were mentioned in Steve's resume document because he thought them unimportant, just "things I do to stay involved."

Highlights of such involvements need to be included on your resume because they tell a story of a more well-rounded and involved you; they help to show how you are curious and engaged in your field beyond just going to work and doing what's required. They show that you have the ability to "get out there" and interact with other professionals. What employer wouldn't want those traits?

What Is a Professional Affiliation?

A professional affiliation is volunteer work or membership to a professional organization that is directly related to your work. In Steve's case, most of his involvement includes professional fundraising organizations or memberships to organizations where he can promote the mission of his workplace.

Steve's examples:

PROFESSIONAL AFFILIATIONS

Association of Fundraising Professionals, Membership Chair (2017 – present);
Member (2010 – present)

Hamilton Chamber of Commerce, Member (2011 – present)

Hamilton Food Bank, Board Member (2008 – 2014)

NOW YOU TRY IT

Identify organizations where you are a member.

1A. _____

2A. _____

3A. _____

What is your role; for example, "member"?

1B. _____

2B. _____

3B. _____

How long you have been involved in that capacity?

1C. _____

2C. _____

3C. _____

Merge each into statements, using the formatting options presented above:

(1A.) _____ (1B.) _____ (1C.) _____

CHAPTER 8

BACKGROUND TO YOUR MASTERPIECE—SHOWCASING YOUR EDUCATION

You might think of the Education section in your resume as the less glamorous, required element. However, the Education section provides information on the foundation of knowledge you bring to your work, where you learned what. Think of it as the drawing you put on paper or canvas before you start painting. That foundation you learned helps to guide the reader in understanding your full knowledge base.

HOW TO MAKE YOUR EDUCATION STAND OUT

Most positions require some level of education beyond high school, whether it is an associate's degree, bachelor's degree, or coursework at the college level. In addition to listing the degree (if applicable), institution, and area of study, include any other activities or important positions you held when participating in activities. Those activities will help to exemplify your history of leadership and high standard of excellence for yourself.

For example:

Bachelor of Arts, Ohio University, Athens Ohio
Major: Communications, with emphasis on Business Communications
Activities: President, Student Alumni Board; Vice President, Delta Delta Delta sorority

Also, think of your education as stretching beyond your college education. In fact, many industries view the training you have beyond high school or college as more relevant to your value in certain positions. For example, any formalized sales training, like Sandler training, is more important for a sales management position than having gotten a communications degree at XYZ University. This is because Sandler training provides a structured and well-known way of approaching sales interactions, with tried-and-true tactics that can be applied immediately to most sales positions. Additional training adds value to you as a candidate. To include that information, list most recent to least recent training you have had.

For example:

EDUCATION and SPECIALIZED TRAINING

Leadership Summit County, Class of 2016

Sandler Sales Training; certified Sandler Train-the-Trainer

Bachelor of Arts in Business and Organizational Communication, Kent State University

Minor in Advertising and Sales

Notice the three ways in which the listing above is different from what you might see on other resumes:

Title of the Section

By including ". . . and Specialized Training" in the title, you prepare the reader for upcoming, specialized information. You indicate that you have skills that are a value-add to the position. For example, "Sandler Sales Training" informs the reader that this candidate has advanced skills in sales, which can certainly differentiate him or her as being more prepared for the position.

No Dates

Leave dates off your education or specialized training entries unless relevant to the position for which you have applied. No one needs to know how old you are. The exception is if a date might align you with a group of people that is desirable, for example, the Leadership Summit County program listed above.

Leadership

Especially when searching for positions within your community, city, or county, participation in leadership programs implies that you have a deeper level of understanding and interest in all aspects of the community. Additionally, these types of programs are outstanding networking environments, which means a candidate with leadership experience might bring more contacts to a new position.

WHAT IF I DON'T HAVE A COLLEGE DEGREE?

David was thinking of pursuing a new position in management. He was worried that his lack of a college degree would get in the way of his ability to move up. In some cases—think medical degree—a degree is very important. But, in many cases, other professional development or specialized programs can replace formal education. David had completed a leadership development program at his existing company and also held Lean Six Sigma certification, which would be valuable as a manager in his field. In David's case, his additional training was more important than a four-year degree received 30 years prior.

Consider the following list of other types of training or non-traditional education that can be listed on your resume:

Coursework Toward a Degree Not Yet Completed

List these classes as "Coursework toward an XYZ degree" and list some of the courses you completed if you think they will be relevant to your story.

Leadership Programs

List internal and external leadership programs in which you have participated. For example, in the city where I live, the local leadership program that the county hosts is very highly regarded and can increase hiring potential.

Specialized Training

Specialized training in your field is highly desirable to potential employers. Assess if there are certain skills or certifications that are advantageous in your field and consider adding that training to your skill base. Then, be sure to list it in your Education and Specialized Training section.

Professional Development (Through Your Company or Independently)

Many companies offer professional development opportunities that some employees think they are too busy to engage in. Make time for these classes, especially if they relate to your longer-term career goals. List the ones you have taken on your resume.

> QUICK TIP
>
> MOST RECENT TO LEAST RECENT
>
> List courses or degrees from most recent to least recent since your most recent professional development will likely be more relevant to the position you are seeking.

NOW YOU TRY IT

Identify education—degrees, coursework, leadership programs, etc.—you have completed.

1A. _____

2A. _____

3A. _____

Through what organization did you receive the education or training?

1B. _____

2B. _____

3B. _____

Are there other details you need to add, like your GPA (if recent and of an accomplished level), "graduated with honors," details about the coursework, etc. Note: you will not have details for all your listings.

1C. _____

2C. _____

3C. _____

Merge each into statements, using the formatting options presented above:

(1A.) _____ (1B.) _____ (1C.) _____

CHAPTER 9

BIGGER CANVAS—HIGHLIGHTING VOLUNTEER AND COMMUNITY INVOLVEMENT

Let's revisit Joanne from a previous chapter. Joanne had very little traditional work experience because she had been busy raising her children. However, she had a great deal of leadership experience and skills cultivated through her volunteer work. In Joanne's case, it was important to list those skills and positions in her Related Experience section because it served as her work experience. Many of my clients participate in community organizations and activities beyond those related to their career but don't think to include that information on their resume.

It's important to include these experiences because they exemplify several things about you:

Your Well-Roundedness
Involvement in community activities are, hopefully, things that you like and choose to do. Inclusion of these details can show your well-roundedness to potential employers; in addition, the kinds of things that interest you beyond your work could turn out to be work-related. For example, you might be an accountant and engage in some pretty specific number crunching by day. In your personal time you participate in a Big Brothers, Big Sisters program. You have no way of knowing if the company where you are interviewing is interested in starting a Junior Achievement program. Your skills in working with and relating to young people may be very desirable.

Your Interest in Contributing to the Good of Your Community
More and more companies are interested in doing good in the community and encouraging employees to be involved in civic-minded activities. Your community activities may indicate that you are a good fit for such a company.

Your Ability to Be a Leader
At your "day job," you may not be in a leadership role or one that allows for recognized leadership opportunities. By listing your roles as a community organization's board of trustees or as the chair of a fundraiser, you show these traits on your resume.

Here are recommendations of what to include and not to include in your community involvement section:

Avoid Controversy

Use common sense and think through how particular activities will be interpreted by potential employers. For example, if you are seeking a position at a pharmaceutical company, a place where animal research sometimes occurs, do not list your involvement with animal support organizations.

Avoid Raising Questions You Don't Want to Answer

Many—most—personal questions are against the law to ask in an interview. Avoid opening the door to those questions by including volunteer activities that invite them. For example, do not list that you are currently the coordinator for a pregnancy support group if you do not want your prospective employer to know you are pregnant (yet).

What to include instead? See the list below:

- Coaching for sports teams

- Involvement in charity fundraisers

- Board of trustee positions

- Leadership in social organizations (sororities, fraternities, Rotary, Kiwanis, etc.)

- Regular volunteering at nonprofits (food banks, ESL support programs, children's support programs, etc.)

- Leadership/involvement in school organizations (PTO/PTA, band boosters, sports boosters, etc.)

Finally, don't include too many details; just give enough information to help the reader understand your interests and involvement. For example:

Susan G. Komen Breast Cancer Foundation of Northeast Ohio, board member, 2015 – present
Battered Women's Shelter Sun County, weekly volunteer work at shelter, 2010 – present
Heritage Elementary School, PTO Membership Chair, 2012 – 2015
Relay for Life, member of team, 2006 – present

NOW YOU TRY IT

Identify roles you have had in your personal life in which you have volunteered or contributed to a cause:

1A. _____

2A. _____

3A. _____

What were the organizations?

1B. _____

2B. _____

3B. _____

What were the years that you volunteered?

1C. _____

2C. _____

3C. _____

Merge each into statements, using the formatting options presented above:

(1A.) _____ (1B.) _____ (1C.) _____

CHAPTER 10

COMPLETING YOUR COMPOSITION—PUTTING IT ALL TOGETHER

Now is the time to step back and review your work of art—the story of the professional *you* on paper. There are some last details to add to your composition:

Add a Discreet Header on Your Second (and Third) Page

Use the "Header and Footer" tool in your word processing software to create a header that lists your *first initial, last name,* and *page sequence* of the second (and third, if needed) pages of your resume. For example:

R. Smith page 2 of 2

Avoid using your header from the first page—the one with your contact information—as it will disrupt reading flow and take up too much space. The limited information above will help the reader reunite your pages if they are separated.

Proofread Your Resume for Typos

A typo on your resume is still the number one reason you will be removed from consideration. In this age of spellcheck, there is no excuse for typos. However, spellcheck will not always catch everything that is inaccurate. I recommend carefully proofreading your document … and then doing it again … and then having someone else proofread it for you. Enlist a friend or family member who has a sharp eye. Ask that person to read your document through thoroughly, once to ensure it is clear and reads well, and a second time to find any typos.

Print Your Resume to See How It Looks

In this day of digital, we all do a lot of reading on screens, so it is important your resume look cohesive, professional, well-designed, and easy-to-read on a screen. Also, print the document to assess for the same attributes. When submitted to a potential employer, your document may very well be shared within a department or across levels of an organization. Ensure it looks equally impressive to all readers!

Save Your Resume as a Portable Document Format (PDF)

Once your resume reads and looks exactly how you want it to, save it as a PDF. A PDF is the only way to ensure your document will look the same across different computer platforms. Also, a PDF will ensure your font will appear exactly as you want it to on your resume.

QUICK TIP

PROOFREAD LIKE A PROFESSIONAL

Professional proofreaders often read text backward, word by word, to make certain all words are spelled correctly. Start at the end of your document with the last word, and read right to left, then bottom to top for a thorough proofing.

CHAPTER 11

EMERGING ARTISTS—GUIDELINES FOR SOON-TO-BE OR RECENT COLLEGE GRADUATES

Congratulations! You are about to enter the "real world." You might be feeling some anxiety about what the future holds for you. We have all been there. I challenge you to find someone—even among those who knew where they were headed professionally post-college—who felt completely confident about job seeking after earning a degree. Add the challenge of creating a resume that will best sell your potential, and you might be tempted to sign up for that fifth year or additional degree program. But the real world is exciting! For good or bad, you finally get to make your own choices for your future! You also get to choose how you want to paint your professional picture on your resume.

Much of the preceding information in Chapters 1 through 10 regarding content will apply to your resume, but you will have some additional, special considerations as to how to best present yourself on paper.

PRINCIPLES FOR EFFECTIVENESS—COLLEGE EDITION

The Flow of the Information and Sections on Your Resume Will Be Different
The flow of your resume sections will most likely differ from those of someone who has been in the working world for a while. Your section flow might look like this:

FLOW #1	OR	FLOW #2
Profile		Profile
Education & Related Coursework		Leadership Activities
Leadership Activities		Awards and Honors
Awards and Honors		Education & Related Coursework
Related Experience		Related Experience
Other Experience		Other Experience

Both flows are geared toward painting a positive picture of your work ethic, accomplishments, and foundational knowledge through coursework/degree work before sharing information about your work experience. Samples of two different college resume formats, one representing a more traditional flow and the other representing a special flow of sections, are included in Chapter 13.

Note This Exception

If you graduate from college with substantial work experience in the field in which you are looking, use the section flow presented in Chapters 2 through 10.

Education and Coursework Can Be More Detailed with Information About Your Courses and Activities

In college, what you have learned and experienced in your classes can certainly supplement, and sometimes replace, real-world work experience. Provide details about any coursework you have taken or leadership positions you have held relevant to the employment you are seeking.

For example:

> **EDUCATION and SPECIALIZED TRAINING**
> **The College of Wooster**
> Bachelor of Arts in Speech Language Pathology and Audiology
> Graduated cum laude
>
> Awards – Dean's List, *Sigma Alpha Tau* English honorary, Varsity Athlete in Girls Basketball
>
> **Other related coursework,** Case Western Reserve University
> Introduction to Neuroscience
> Articulation and Phonology
> Adolescent Psychology

Include Any Awards and Honors You Have Received

Receiving awards and being honored speaks volumes about your work ethic and leadership potential. These distinctions might not seem important to you when you are job seeking, but providing information about them on your resume will help a future employer gauge your leadership potential. For example:

> **AWARDS AND HONORS**
>
> Outstanding Senior Leader Award (2017 – 2018)
>
> Student Commencement Speaker (2018)
>
> The Torch Award (2017 – 2018) in recognition of dedication to Student Alumni Board
>
> Emerging Greek Leader (2016 – 2017)
>
> Ohio University Dean's List (2014 – 2018)

Merge Your Paid and Unpaid Experience, Using "Related Experience" and "Other Experience" as Your Experience Section Headers

Correctly organizing your comprehensive work experience, paid and unpaid, will allow you to tell the most cohesive story about your relevant experience. For example, Callie is seeking a post-graduation position working outdoors and utilizing her environmental science degree. Her Experience sections look like this:

Related Experience

Buck-i-SERV, Columbus, Ohio   Spring Break 2015, 2016, 2018
Volunteer

- Installed roof rafters on a Habitat for Humanity build site in Lake Sumter, FL

- Participated in coral reef and wetland restoration in Hammock's Beach State Park, NC

- Built enclosure for rescued red pandas in Silver Springs, FL

Westhaven Country Club   Summer 2015, 2017
Grounds Crew Member

- Acted as team lead of summer interns tasked with maintaining, grooming, and repairing golf course grounds

- Learned how to and provided care for specialized plants and rare grass varieties on the course

- Recognized by superiors for dependability and superb attention to detail, promoted to maintaining greens and rough

Other Experience

The Cheesecake Factory   September 2017 – present
Senior Team Member/Line Cook

- Provides excellent customer service; coached and motivated 10-member team at company's flagship restaurant by instituting an employee engagement program

- Responsibilities include taking customer orders, preparing food, managing inventory, and executing cash register duties; promoted to catering, nightly closer, and trainer of new employees

- Demonstrates strong interpersonal and customer communication skills daily

Hamilton Bank   Summer 2016
Intern

- Served as intern team lead in digitizing and organizing customer files, improving retrieval times, and reducing bank operating costs

If You Don't Have Much "Work Experience" or "Related Experience," Dig Deeply into Your Course Experiences

Use the content and experiences of your courses or extra projects as "work" experience. If structured well by a professor, a class group project in college or other research or study project is similar to a group project experience in a work environment. Likewise, some additional college experiences will be directly applicable to the work you are seeking. For example, research in the sciences is often the same research you would be doing in a work environment and can be presented like this:

Biology Student Researcher, Ashland University, Ashland, OH   8/2016 – present
- Assists professor's research in isolating bacteria from various water supplies, whose metabolic properties allow them to use estrogen as an energy source

- Performs various biological laboratory techniques, such as DNA extraction, polymerase chain reaction, gel electrophoresis, and bacterial culture techniques

- Interprets and records data

Biology Laboratory Technician, Ashland University, Ashland, OH   8/2015 – 5/2017
- Cares for laboratory mice, including feeding and changing bedding

- Waters plants in the university greenhouse; cleans the greenhouse on a weekly schedule

- Makes and prepares various types of growth media for use by different professors

- Cleans and organizes various biology supplies for university department

To recap, although you will be able to use much of the information about *content* in the previous chapters, you will want to *organize* the information differently, as described in this chapter, to have a resume that speaks to who you are and where you are headed.

Now go out and conquer the world!

QUICK TIP

LISTING OF DATES

In most resumes, I recommend *not* listing dates for education and training. No one needs to know how old you are, just what experience and skills you have. However, in the case of a recent graduate, it can often work in your favor to let a potential employer know you are new to the field. Showing your "newness," will help explain your lack of direct experience in a field and will potentially encourage that employer to take a chance on you.

CHAPTER 12

VOILÀ! YOUR WORK OF ART IS COMPLETE! NOW WHAT?

Stephen had worked diligently on his resume. He felt proud of the document he created and the professional story it presented about him. At the end of our appointment he looked at me and said, "Now what?"

Now it was time for him to start the job application process. Although this step is beyond the scope of this book, and much information is available elsewhere, here are some tips to the most frequently asked questions about this step:

FAQs FOR THE JOB APPLICATION PROCESS

Cover Letter or Not?
Many postings will not list a cover letter as a requirement for applying to a position, but here is the main reason to include one: A cover letter is a great opportunity to expand on your story with information that isn't included on your resume. It is the place to share a particular reason why you are applying to the position or company. By telling an engaging story, you encourage someone to read further and view your resume.

For positions that require a written communication component, a cover letter serves as a writing sample and showcases your comfort and expertise with the written word. For positions that don't require a written component, a well-written cover letter makes you look more professional and well-spoken than your competitors. Who doesn't want the better communicator on his or her team?

Each of the points above will make you memorable, and hiring managers call unique candidates to learn more about them.

A Few Cover Letter Pointers
Find a specific person to address your letter to; if you don't know the name of the person who will be doing the hiring, choose "Dear HR Representative" or "Dear Hiring Manager."

Keep your cover letter simple, but add keywords from the posting that will help the reader picture you in the position. Align your skills with the desirable qualities listed in the position description, but don't feel you have to list everything. Choose the most important qualifications. Determine importance by seeing how many times a skill or quality is mentioned in the posting.

Don't give everything away in your cover letter; use phrases to drive the reader to your resume to see your full professional story. For example, "Having worked at one of the most well-known companies specializing in software solutions, I achieved #1 sales person for my region 4 years in a row." This kind of wording will leave the reader wanting to know what company and when you worked there.

Try to find a unique story or reason why you are applying to the specific position and want to work for the company. I once interviewed a candidate for a position because, in his cover letter, he shared that he owned an outdoor survival school. It was relevant to the job, and I wanted to know more, so I called him for an interview.

Include your contact information—phone and email—in the last paragraph of your letter. You do not want someone having to hunt for your contact information if he or she wants to call you for an interview.

Sign off professionally with "Sincerely" or "Best Regards."

Keep your letter to three to four paragraphs on one page. Your resume will provide the details.

Whom Do I Choose for References?

Plan to have four to six individuals who say good, meaningful things about your work. Consider asking a former supervisor, coworker, or a client who loves your work and whom you trust. Ask at the start of your job seeking, so each person will be already thinking about nice things to say about you and your work prior to getting an email or call.

Since most applications and hiring managers no longer ask for references with your resume, be prepared to provide the list of your references when you are asked for them. You can provide references on paper or by email, with name, title, company or organization, phone number, and email. Contact each reference when this is requested so he or she will be ready if contacted by the hiring professional.

How Do I Navigate the Online Application Systems (aka the Dreaded "Bots")?

Applicant Tracking Systems (ATS) are used by approximately 95% of Fortune 500 companies, and are widely used by other organizations as well. These systems are brutal at weeding out resumes that don't match the preloaded criteria for positions.

Here are some quick tips on how to make the ATS cut:

Keywords, Keywords, Keywords

When you submit a resume through an online ATS, your document is generally given a "match" score. The higher the number of the match, the more likely your materials are to be forwarded to the next step and seen by a person. Your match score is dependent on the number of words you have on your document that match the words that have been entered into the ATS, generally words that have been selected from the posting. TagCrowd is a great online service that allows you to input a posting; it will create a word cloud that shows what words are emphasized in it. Remember the keyword match that was discussed in Chapter 4? Here is where it really matters. The better match you have with the posting, the more likely you are to be contacted. Period.

Don't Over Format

The ATS doesn't like "fancy." Save your beautiful design for resumes you deliver via email or in-person. Elaborate formatting will "confuse" the ATS, and your resume will be removed from consideration. The recommendations I have made throughout the previous chapters will work with ATS.

Logos, pictures, and fancy/hard-to-read fonts are some typical items that an ATS will not understand. Other tips are to avoid unusual characters—the ATS doesn't like symbols such as ampersands (&) and other "fussy" characters. Likewise, use language for your sections that the ATS understands, like "Profile," "Skills," "Experience." While "Core Competencies" has become fashionable in some industries, and that title has its proper place, an ATS most likely will not understand that your competencies are skills.

Complete All the Fields

It is important to fill out all of the fields in an ATS. Every once in a while a client contacts me and states, "I don't want to put a salary range on my application because it might prevent me from getting an interview. They might not be able to afford me." I understand the reasoning, but the ATS bots really don't like blank fields and your application might get kicked out of the system. Think of the ATS as your high school social studies teacher who didn't like blank answers on a test; do your research (for salary ranges use salary.com or glassdoor.com) and fill in the complete application.

Follow-up

Follow-up serves as "doing an end run" around ATS bots. Your application process should not end once you hit "send" and apply for the desired position. Follow-up can make the difference between getting a call for the interview or not. Once your application is complete and sent, I suggest emailing a PDF copy of your resume and cover letter to the person you think will be your supervisor (or know, if lucky enough to have it listed in the posting) with a short note expressing your interest in the position and stating that you want to ensure that a person has a chance to review your materials. There are several ways you can try to discover who your supervisor would be:

Prospect Your LinkedIn Connections

You never know who knows whom, and you can use the LinkedIn search feature to find connections who may have a link to the person you are seeking. Enter the company name into the search bar and hit "return." The result will provide 1st, 2nd, and 3rd degree connections who are associated with that company through current or past work, or a LinkedIn connection of their own. Once you have that list, determine the best contact for your needs. I recommend filtering your search results by 1st or 2nd degree connections since those people will be most easy for you to access.

Look at the Company's Website

Organizations provide a wealth of information on staffing structure. If you are not sure who your supervisor would be, look on the organization's website for a staff listing. Often this listing will not appear in the main body of the website, especially if the company deals in any kind of consumer product. Instead, you can often find this information in the small print section of the website, located in the footer. Search for the person you think would be your supervisor. For example, if you are applying for a marketing position, look for a Director of Marketing.

Search Via a Web Browser for Your Best Guess of Your Supervisor

Using the example above, type "Director of Marketing at XYZ Company" into an Internet browser. See what pops up. Finding that person's contact information might be as easy as that!

Search for a Company's Organizational Chart

An organizational chart or "org chart" is a graphical or written overview of the leadership and staffing structure of a company. In a web browser, search "XYZ Company organizational chart." You can get a lot of junk regarding org charts in general, but sometimes you can strike gold and find a result for that specific company, listing who is in charge of what responsibilities. In a pinch, send your follow-up materials to the HR Director or the CEO of a company if it's a smaller company. The most important thing is to try to get your materials into the hands of a living person, as well as a computer!

WHAT IS THE FUTURE OF RESUMES?

There has been much talk about the future of resumes, especially in this digital and screen-driven age. Great speculation exists as to whether or not the paper resume will be disappearing. Video resumes, where candidates present their attributes, skills, and work history in a brief verbal and visual presentation, are starting to pop up on platforms such as LinkedIn and YouTube. There has even been discussion via blogs and articles about global search systems that will extensively search all online outlets for any information regarding a candidate, making recruiters aware of a potential candidate before that person is even considering a new position.

The common thought is that traditional paper resumes will not disappear anytime soon. You will definitely need an overview on paper to hand out at an interview. A good resume is a great way to provide a favorable professional representation of your work history. It is also still an ideal way to organize your information in a concise format.

Your qualifications and work history will be reviewed by individuals of varying ages and technology savviness. A paper resume offers everyone accessibility to your information. Lastly, have you ever had to click through several online pages to get to the content you are seeking? It's annoying, right? A paper resume provides "one-stop shopping" for your information with no click-throughs.

However, having made a case for the paper resume, your document is best augmented by other tools, such as a very good LinkedIn profile or a link you can list on your resume of a short video of the best traits and skills you bring to the table. Think integration of available technology.

FINAL WORDS

Most importantly, do not forget the job search is a marathon, not a 10K. Arm yourself with the right materials, pace yourself, and make room for fun, non-job-related activities during your search. Finding the right next position often takes time, but fulfilling work or an exciting new career is out there for you! Life is too short to be unhappy at work! Take your time to find the perfect fit for you.

CHAPTER 13

SAMPLE RESUMES

Sample Hybrid Resume

Sample Hybrid Resume – Executive Format

Sample Hybrid Resume – Alternative Executive Format

Sample Hybrid Resume – Nontraditional Work Experience Format

Sample Hybrid Resume – College Student / Recent Graduate Format

Sample Hybrid Resume – Alternate Format for Recent College Graduate

Steve Johnson

linkedin.com/in/stevejohnson

sjohnsonshrm@gmail.com • 412-555-5555

Human Resources Management Professional / Specializing in Talent Acquisition and Training

PROFILE

Entrepreneurial human resources manager with experience in all aspects of recruiting and developing teams and talent, within for-profit and non-profit global organizations • Drives and delivers solid measurable results and builds strong professional networks • Independently sets direction and prioritizes activities to deliver on organizational goals • Adept at coaching, influencing, and motivating individuals and teams to achieve success and the organization's vision, mission, and strategies • Known for a passion for delivering high quality work and thriving under pressure, focusing on results

SKILLS

- **Human Resources Knowledge** – certified and experienced in the execution of most Human Resource practices, including talent acquisition and retention; employee engagement, learning and development; rewards and recognition; workforce management; diversity and inclusion; risk management; social responsibility; employment laws and regulations

- **Talent Acquisition, Management, Team Building and Leadership** – proven ability to lead, coach, and empower a successful team of high performing support staff; exceptional skills in motivating teams and maintaining high-levels of staff loyalty; specialized recruitment expertise in sourcing, qualifying, job analysis, salary trends and relationship management

- **Society of Human Resources Management (SHRM) Certified** – past positions of leadership in the SHRM State Council, an affiliate of the Society for Human Resource Management; led 25 SHRM Chapters and over 300 volunteer leaders who serve on chapter board of directors; informs chapters on changes in HR law and protocol; acts as strategic advisor to chapter presidents

- **Technical Skills**- knowledge of MS Office suite software including Microsoft Word, Publisher, PowerPoint, Excel, Access; experience with Applicant Tracking Systems, including Taleo, Ceridian, and Kronos; proficient at Salesforce and other CRM software; utilizes Google – Drive, Slides, Docs, Sheets and Hangouts

PROFESSIONAL EXPERIENCE

Human Resources Manager   2007 – present
Staffing Solutions

- Leads the vision, strategy, and execution for all facets of operations throughout Northeast Ohio, including staffing needs for 12 corporate accounts requiring 5-10 positions filled monthly

- Executes strategic planning, market research, financial analysis, operating budgets, contract negotiations, recruitment strategies, and marketing strategies

- Exercises responsibility for over $8M in P&L with a continuous record of success in driving revenues and improving bottom line profit performance

- Heads talent acquisition, management, training and development, employee engagement, general Human Resources oversight, workforce planning, and forecasting

- Designs and implements sourcing and full cycle recruiting strategies, marketing campaigns, social media strategies, budgets and forecasts to achieve talent pipeline and job order fulfillment goals

- Engages in workforce planning to position the company to readily meet the needs of client companies across multiple functional areas, including warehousing, customer service, contact center, accounting, manufacturing, semi-skilled and skilled labor, office and administration, human resources and business professional services
- Developed and strengthened relationships and strategic partnerships with executives and other key stakeholders within clients and prospects, positioning the company as a trusted strategic partner invested in the success of its customers

Key Accomplishments

Selected by President of company to **serve on a select team of specialized trainers** to provide national support to team leads of a new service delivery model roll-out for company-wide training

Winner of company's **Circle of Stars Award 2011, 2012, 2015 and 2017**

Selected by corporate Human Resources of global staffing company to **conduct new hire orientation for North America staff new hires**, as well as provide best practices

Human Resources Specialist   2002 – 2007
Excel Company

- Recruited, oriented and trained staff for manufacturing company with 250-325 employees during tenure working there
- Scheduled and attended networking events and hiring events to recruit new staff
- Implemented unique employee engagement and recognition program; cut employee absenteeism by 40% and employee turnover by 15%
- Researched and introduced new benefits provider which the company subsequently adopted at a cost reduction of approximately 35%
- Helped to produce yearly Human Resources department operating budgets

Additional foundational experience as Human Resources Generalist in the manufacturing industry.

EDUCATION and SPECIALIZED TRAINING

SHRM Certified Professional in Human Resources (SHRM-CP)
Society for Human Resource Management – Pittsburgh, PA

Bachelor of Science in Business Administration, specializing in Human Resources
Duquesne University – Pittsburgh, PA

PROFESSIONAL AFFILIATIONS

Pennsylvania SHRM State Council, an Affiliate of the Society for Human Resource Management

State Director	January 2018 – December 2019
Director-Elect	January 2017 – December 2017
Membership Director	January 2014 – December 2016

SHRM – Butler County, an Affiliate of the Society for Human Resource Management

President	January 2013 – December 2013
VP Membership	January 2012 – December 2012
President-Elect/VP Programs	January 2011 – December 2011

Carrie Smith

2120 Wellville Road, Happytown, Ohio 44444 ♦ (216) 555-5555 ♦ csmith@gmailmba.com

Sales Management Executive / Specialization in Medical Device

CAREER PROFILE

Goal-driven, loyal sales management leader with award winning performance in program development and sales direction in the medical device industry ♦ Capably listens to customer needs, ask probing questions and creates customized selling techniques utilizing consultative selling process and Sandler Training ♦ Drives the sales process by initiating collaborative team management which helps team members create customer buy-in, initiating forward action ♦ Highly accountable to teams, organizational heads, and stakeholders; comfortably communicates across the selling continuum including C-level executives

QUALIFICATIONS and SKILLS

- **Strategic Marketing and Launch Expertise-** exhibits exemplary performance in opportunity identification, product demonstration and group presentation, especially related to project launch; skilled at bringing, introducing, and growing new technology in the marketplace

- **Continuous Process Improvement-** highly adept at assisting clients in building programs to address the changing marketplace, continually developing solutions, initiatives and new processes to ensure customers view relationship as that of strategic business partner

- **Technical Support-** high degree of technical aptitude, providing consultative support to ensure technology is being properly utilized; advanced training in Salesforce and implementation plans

- **Quality Assurance and Regulatory Compliance-** participates as a trusted business partner on relevant standards committees to help ensure product compliance with industry standards and regulatory requirements

- **Leadership, Training, and Team Building-** calls upon an in-depth background in on-site teaching and in-servicing to drive training and team performance

SELECT AWARDS and RECOGNITION

Ranked #1 representative overall 2017; ranked #2 representative overall 2018 at Healthy Heart Medical Care

Honored in companies' Presidents Club 2017, 2015, 2014, 2012 and 2011 as top 10% sales representative in nation (Healthy Heart Medical Care, Optimal Healthcare and Certified Medical Devices)

Received Recognition in Optimal Healthcare's "100% Club" for 2015 sales (110%)

Received Optimal Healthcare's 2014 Manager's Choice Award for outstanding performance and dedication

PROFESSIONAL EXPERIENCE

Director of Business Development   2016 – present
Healthy Heart Medical Care – Happytown, OH
- Directs all aspects of developing new therapy programs aimed at the heart failure population; monitors and encourages continuous growth of therapy; manages therapy growth within 10 major accounts
- Proactively partners with hospitals to implement new therapy programs within a Shared Risk Model that addresses CMS Readmission Incentives; provides prompt, comprehensive field support regarding application and use of therapy

- Provides clinical resource guidance including assistance with clinical protocol/procedure development and ongoing program and clinical literature review; consults on recommendations for using new therapy, reviewing data and guidelines in program
- Strengthens quality and outcome data reviews; encourages and supports the hospital in review of relevant quality and outcome data to develop potential improvements
- Increased therapy utilization by 40% by continually monitoring projects within the customer organization keeping focus on therapy growth while being viewed as trusted business partner

Territory Manager   2012 – 2016
Optimal Healthcare – Columbus, OH
- Worked within the medical community, selling to multidisciplinary committees—from C-Suite, Cardiologists, Nurse Managers, Nurse Educators, Nursing Administration, to Bedside Nurses—to obtain client base for market development of new product that offers a novel approach to the chronic and costly problem that plagues heart failure patients
- Executed in a wide array of roles, including developing and shaping in-service protocols and tools needed in the field, troubleshooting during patient treatments, increasing utilization within territories, and obtaining new prescribers of therapy
- Responsible for identifying new targets and prospecting revenue channels; nurtured loyal following of comprehensive staff within the Cardiology/Heart Failure community
- As a Territory Manager worked with 20 accounts in strategizing sales calls, product demonstration, and marketing activities that helped to maximize corporate profitability and sales
- Conducted training with medical team, including physicians and nurses, on clinical indications and the use of device by providing comprehensive in-service sessions and resolving any concerns and issues that arise
- Cultivated in-depth knowledge of CMS Reimbursement Changes and ACO Initiatives
- Performed as a National Field Trainer, growing territory from $750K to $1.5M annually in 4 years

Account Representative, Northeast and Central Ohio   2005 – 2012
Certified Medical Devices – Philadelphia, PA
- Reliably developed relationships with key decision makers in the Operating Room, Critical Care, Medsurg and Materials Management for Northeast and Central Ohio sales territory
- Accountable for sales of 2 new product lines while maintaining existing business in existing products
- Fostered relationships and successfully worked with wide variety of doctors including Orthopedic, General, Neurology and Vascular Surgeons to secure sales, grow market and develop existing business
- Obtained in-depth knowledge of all major GPOs; cultivated strong distributor relationships
- Met all corporate target and sales goals each year while managing 5th largest sales territory in company

EDUCATION and ADDITIONAL TRAINING

Master of Business Administration with an emphasis on nursing homes and gerontology
The Ohio State University, Columbus, OH

Bachelor of Arts, Communications Major
Kent State University, Kent, OH

VOLUNTEER and COMMUNITY INVOLVEMENT

Member, National Association of Professional Women, 2014 – present
Board Member, The Ohio State University Alumni Association, 2014 – 2018
Race Team Coordinator, Relay For Life, 2010 – 2015
Regularly participates/donates to multiple charities, including the local food banks and Make-a-Wish Foundation

JULIE WILSON

www.linkedin.com/in/juliewilson

JulieWilson604@gmail.com • 330.555.5555

Media Advertising Executive / Specializing in Operations Maximization and Growth

PROFILE

Positive, high energy business development and market expansion leader with deep and diverse industry experience in Media and Advertising, including Print, Digital Marketing, Radio, TV, Cable, and e-Commerce technologies • Recognized for thought leadership, capably solving problems methodically from development through execution and control • Cultivates proven strategy within team and is driven by efficient, analytical decision-making utilizing qualitative and quantitative data • Collaborator and empathetic listener who is also successful at building strong relationships across all areas of the company and the industry

SKILLS

- **Relationship Management** – Ultimate connector and collaborator; strong networking and community involvement skills; applies focused listening, analyzing clients' needs to understand their business and then designs effective solutions, maximizing their investment

- **Negotiation** – Professional, articulate and focused negotiator who approaches situations with the goal of accomplishing best-case outcomes for all parties; experienced and comfortable negotiating with independent operators to C-level executives; relied upon for results and win-win scenarios

- **Change Management / Vision** – Leads transformation and inspires change while maintaining the integrity and respect for traditional and established processes; effectively encourages clients to take on new technology and new ways of reaching audiences; able to solve problems logically and methodically with great creativity

- **Sales Strategy** – Expert at understanding clients' needs within existing business and then designs successful solutions, maximizing client goals in meeting sales targets; excellent at connecting products to solutions that match goals

- **Team Management** – Nurtures long-term professional development of team members; highly intuitive in understanding each member's drive and mentors team members with appropriate, differentiated techniques; models eagerness to learn, continually seeking to improve sales skills and the skills of others

PROFESSIONAL EXPERIENCE

Director, National Account Strategy   2017 – present
All-In Media, Inc.

- Cultivates relationships with key media executives at the local, regional and corporate levels, by successfully building rapport and providing strategies for success
- Communicates the value proposition of products, seamlessly onboarding new clients; sets and exceeds expectations for customers and company
- Successfully executes enterprise-wide relationships; effectively sells the entire suite of SaaS technology solutions to top media companies, including iHeartMedia and more
- Drives and models consultative, customer-centric selling behaviors; presents solutions which are appropriate to client needs and constantly monitors the health of the relationship and products; collaborates with the Partner Success team to address the needs, opportunities and challenges of client partners
- Effectively collaborates with management to provide detailed revenue forecast and market/company intelligence; knowledge of competitive media landscape, used for new business development and sales analysis

Key Accomplishment

Increased national market share by 30% in first 8 months

Director of Business Development 2010 – 2017
Quality Manufacturing, LLC

- Successfully developed and managed 6 regional sales managers, sales support members and web teams; exercised ability to recognize talented individuals and mentor each to successful career opportunities, all while aggressively moving the goals of the company forward
- Created and improved operational systems, processes and policies in support of the company's mission to include enhanced management reporting; upgraded internal communication processes and progressive organizational planning; coordinated RFPs, contracts and execution in collaboration with legal department
- Developed marketing efforts that complimented sales activities, including updating company website; led efforts to build automated tools and triggers such as landing pages, video campaigns, integrated marketing campaigns for lead generation and social media campaigns to align with marketing campaigns

Key Accomplishment

Effectively built key business with direct increase to the company's revenue by an average of 15% per year; oversaw budget of $6M yearly

Sales Manager 2005 – 2010
All-Pro Services

- Collaborated with the company's leadership team in the development of improved and new solutions that increased the overall value proposition in the marketplace; grew regional market share by 20% in the first 2 years
- Devised and implemented sales training webinars/programs for new clients and re-engagement campaigns for existing clients
- Identified areas of improvement for partners and established processes for enhancing overall revenue performance; prospected and built sales pipeline for new product sales while nurturing and developing third party relationships; identified areas of improvement for partners, establishing processes for improving overall revenue

Key Accomplishment

Maximized revenue and profitability for the company by achieving revenue plans, increased the overall number of clients from 150 to 350 and developed marketing strategies for overall growth

Director of Sales 2000 – 2005
Hamilton Daily

- Managed a team of 5 outside sales executives; increased advertising revenues by 20% in year 1 by actively engaging with clients independently or by collaborating with team in sales calls and client visits
- Created incentive programs for the sales team's department; implemented weekly meetings and reviewed performance to goals, new business opportunities and challenges
- Hosted a three-time annual event with national exposure, local entertainment and sold out venues; each event generated over $50K in revenue from ticket sales, booth sales, advertising in the new special edition and sponsorships

Additional foundational experience at Stark Advertising, ABC Advertising, and Harrison Advertising

EDUCATION

Leadership Hamilton County, 2016

Bachelor of Arts in Business and Communication, College of Wooster
Minor in Advertising and Sales; Speech and Rhetoric

VOLUNTEER and COMMUNITY INVOLVEMENT

Hamilton Area Chamber of Commerce, Member, 2005 – present
American Red Cross, *Board Member, 2015 – 2017*
United Way of Hamilton County, *Board Member, 2006 – 2012*

Joanne Silver

330-421-9552 ♦ jsilver720@gmail.com

PROFILE

Capable and committed community engagement leader and program developer with diverse events management, membership development and fundraising experience ♦ Recognized for building high-quality, sought-after events that raise awareness and exceed fundraising goals ♦ Known for bringing together groups of people to accomplish projects creatively and efficiently ♦ Adept at accomplishing tasks or delegating; depending on what situations require ♦ Works well leading diverse groups of people and gaining consensus on direction, project plans, tasks order and project outcomes

SKILLS

Event Planning – Adept at conceptualizing and executing all aspects of special events, including location acquisition, vendor selection, catering arrangements, coordinating live and silent auctions, volunteer recruitment, and oversight of financial management; events has ranged in size from 50 to 800 attendees

Fundraising – Accomplished at raising funds for a variety of organizations; familiar with diverse fundraising strategies, including direct appeals, letter writing appeals, auctions, raffles, and sponsorships; comfortable approaching different types of donors

Public Speaking – Easily engages in public speaking, especially when related to a cause; appropriately messages urgency and need of issues, appealing to a wide range of donors or members

Scheduling and Timeline Management – Applies advanced skills in scheduling and timeline oversight; very organized; able to track and schedule out a variety of tasks, often happening simultaneously

Volunteer Management – Deep experience recruiting, training and directing large groups of volunteers, for events or independent tasks; accustomed to working with boards of trustees as well as facilitating with paid office staff of organizations

RELATED EXPERIENCE

Membership Chair 2016 – present
Hamilton High School Band Boosters
- Oversees and coordinates recruitment efforts for 200-member support organization; increased membership 25% in first year
- Provides orientation to new members which includes explaining committee options and purpose of each, pairing each new member with a mentor and serving as the point person for any questions
- Attends other high school events as a representative of the group, sharing information on purpose and involvement

Event Chairwoman 2012 – 2015
The Red Heart Ball for Heart Health, First General Hospital
- Coordinated yearly gala with attendance up to 800 and raising between $150-250K annually
- Oversaw all aspects of the event, including sponsors, live and silent auction volunteers, ambassador donors program and facilitation with honorary guest chairs
- Met with hospital staff to recruit important medically-relevant expert attendees for the event
- Promoted event via many community outlets, including providing information on live radio interviews
- Solicited high visibility guest emcees or honorary chairs of national fame

President/Vice President/Secretary, Hamilton PTO 2005 – 2012
Hamilton Elementary School

- Served in progressive leadership roles for the school support organization that ranged in size from 25 to 40 members
- Oversaw monthly projects, including Terrific Tuesday meals for teachers, newsletter for all school parents and guardians and Recycle for Cash program
- Facilitated execution of volunteer-driven special events, including Book Fair, yearly Carnival, Sweets with Santa and yearly Fun Run
- Coordinated with state-wide PTO to achieve compliance with PTO guidelines; attended state conference 5 years in a row

OTHER EXPERIENCE

Officer Manager 2002 – 2004
State Farm Insurance of Hamilton

- Executed administrative tasks for 5 agent insurance office, including tracking schedules, submitting claims, tracking expense reports, and answering client queries
- Oversaw 2 office support staff
- Completed monthly payroll

EDUCATION and SPECIALIZED TRAINING

"Fundraising for Community Members," SCORE (Senior Council of Retired Executives)

Bachelor of Arts Degree, Communications Major, Miami University, Oxford, Ohio

VOLUNTEER INVOLVEMENT

Member and Participant, Hamilton Race for the Cure, 2012 – present
Monthly volunteer, Hamilton County Food Bank, 2010 – 2014
Soccer Coach, Hamilton Youth Recreation League, 2008 – 2012

Mary Madison

216-321-4552   ♦   marymadison@wvu.edu

PROFILE

Highly motivated natural leader and recent graduate who successfully manages team dynamics to achieve organizational goals ♦ Accomplished problem solver with an ability to identify challenges and see them to completion ♦ Quick learner with a desire for continuous personal growth ♦ Exceptional interpersonal skills that can leverage communication to drive results and create a growth environment ♦ Resourceful, flexible professional with the ability to accomplish goals with little guidance or instruction ♦ Capable of absorbing and interpreting large amounts of possibly conflicting information for organizational purposes

SUMMARY OF QUALIFICATIONS AND SKILLS

- **Industry Knowledge** – In-depth understanding of required Long Term Care and administrative practices with an ability to apply to current healthcare environment

- **Administrative Skills** – Broad knowledge of budgets, accounting, and compliance and program development practices

- **Communication** – Concise and fluent communicator, adept at structuring materials and meetings to ensure successful results

- **Human Resources** – Experience in human resource functions such as recruiting, interviewing, hiring, orienting, performance reviews, employee relations, strategic management, and working with boards of directors

- **Technology** – Knowledge of computer software including Microsoft Word, Publisher, Power-Point, Excel, Peachtree accounting software; adept at internet; some knowledge of EPIC

RELATED EXPERIENCE

Administrative, Regional Operations Intern   6/2015 – 8/2015
The Cleveland Clinic – Cleveland, Ohio
- Produced standard operating procedures to be compatible with EPIC and to increase efficiency within daily administrative tasks; disseminated to staff and fielded questions regarding the scheduling system and use
- Assisted in supervising clinical and clerical duties including staff scheduling, physician on boarding, medical concerns, expected service behavior, and value based care
- Collaborated with project team to plan a region wide softball tournament to benefit the American Heart Association; fundraising goal of $7K+ was achieved
- Improved patient experience and decrease wait time through a time study of express care locations

Administrative, Geriatrics Intern   1/2015 – 4/2015
University Medical Associates – Athens, Ohio
- Executed long-term accounting responsibilities such as preparing and entering journal entries for payroll, conducted refunds, allocated benefits, and completed assigned projects; performed daily accounting responsibilities such as paying bills and allocating payments to departments
- Served as a member of the staff development committee; created event survey and review form
- Completed over 5K patient records audits and design presentation boards
- Developed a senior resource guide for the geriatrics department in order to inform patients on available resources within the surrounding area

Teacher Assistant   8/2014 – 12/2014
Ohio University Long Term Care program – Athens, Ohio
- Created projects and assignments for a Human Resources course
- Carried out attendance and grading responsibilities
- Assisted in advising students on their academics

Administrative Intern   6/2012 – 8/2012
Gentle Oaks Nursing Facility – Avon, Ohio
- Completed a 10-week internship designed to provide the knowledge, skills, and competencies required for the long-term healthcare field
- Assisted in supervising clinical and administrative affairs including overseeing staff and personnel, financial matters, medical care, medical supplies, and quality care of over 100 residents
- Facilitated social events for residents including individual or group events, improving quality of life
- Absorbed and interpreted large amounts of possibly conflicting information in order to conduct chart and physician file audits

RELATED STUDENT INVOLVEMENT

Member   10/2012 – 5/2015
American College of Healthcare Administrators
- Nationwide professional society dedicated to advancing the standards of long term care
- Increased student engagement by promoting involvement in campus-wide functions that reinforced the importance of long term care
- Facilitated networking sessions with alumni, allowing members to gain purposeful relationships

President   3/2015 – 5/2015
Vice President of Alumni Engagement   3/2013 – 3/2015
Member   2/2012 – 5/2012
Student Alumni Board
- Professional organization dedicated to establishing and enhancing connections between current students and alumni by creating programs and opportunities to encourage these relationships
- Coordinated and supervised all activities for a 90 member, 8 committee organization including alumni networking, professional development, and philanthropic events
- Acted as liaison to the Ohio University Alumni Association and campus-wide Counsel of Student Leaders in order to ensure a presence on and off campus

EDUCATION

Bachelor of Science in Health, Ohio University, 2015
   Major: Health Services Administration, Long Term Care; Minor: Business Administration
   Certificate in Gerontology; GPA: 3.728/4.0

AWARDS AND HONORS

Outstanding Senior Leader Award (2014 – 2015) **Student Commencement Speaker** (2015)
The Torch Award (2013 – 2014) in recognition of dedication to Student Alumni Board
Emerging Greek Leader (2011 – 2012)   **Ohio University Dean's List** (2011 – 2015)

VOLUNTEER, COMMUNITY, AND OTHER STUDENT INVOLVEMENT

Alumnae Relations Chair, Alpha Delta Pi Sorority (8/2013 – 4/2015)
Co-chair, Student Philanthropy Initiative (8/2014 – 5/2015)
OHIO Women Making a Difference Conference committee member, Women in Philanthropy (2012 –2015)

John Mason

1101 Happy Lane
Happytown, Ohio 44256
Masonjkgmail.com
216-444-1212

PROFILE

Hardworking and highly responsible Library Sciences major with experience in multiple community settings • Exceptional social skills working with diverse individuals • Excels at creating new and innovative programming and solutions, especially those related to digital libraries • Actively engages in and volunteers for tasks; detail oriented yet is flexible and adapts to changing situations • Takes initiative when working independently or in a group setting

EDUCATION

Combined Bachelor's and Master's Library and Information Science Degree,
Kent State University, Kent, Ohio, 2018
> Select specialized coursework- The Information Landscape; People in the Information Ecology; Digital Technologies I, II, and II; Metadata Architecture and Implementation; Cultural Heritage Informatics
> GPA- 3.8

Post-Secondary Classes at Cuyahoga Community College, 1/2013 – 5/2014
> Select classes- Spanish 5 & 6, Psychology 1 & 2, Sociology, Communications

LEADERSHIP ACTIVITIES

American Library Association (ALA) Student Chapter
> Member (2014 – 2018); Membership Chair (2016 – 2018)

Ambassador, iSchool (School of Information)
> Led tours and information sessions for prospective students to iSchool programs

AWARDS and HONORS

> **Dean's List**, 2014 – 2018 (all years attending program)

> **Luce Memorial Scholarship Recipient**, awarded to a Senior in the Digital Libraries program

RELATED EXPERIENCE

Stark County District Library – Kent, Ohio   2015 – 2018
> **Research Assistant/Intern** (2016 – 2018)
- Assisted patrons with data requests, including online program information, GED location and testing information and job seeking assistance
- Supported Reference and Nonfiction Department Librarians and Associates in patron requests
- Attended annual Research Librarian meetings for updated procedures and customer service policies
- Used SIRSI to change book statuses with in the ClevNet system
- Attended ALA National Conference; presented a poster session on new data technologies

Nonfiction Department Intern (2015 – 2016)
- Assisted with library programs, author visits, holiday events, other special events including, Find Your Family, Your Numbers Count and What's New in Nonfiction
- Assisted patrons in special requests regarding research projects; presented information at local high schools to introduce "The New Digital Library" to students
- Cleaned old books and accessed new books
- Organized and displayed books within the Department
- Assisted Librarians in new book selection

Cleveland Heights – University Heights Public Library   2011 – 2014
Page
- Shelved returned items to their proper locations within the library
- Assisted members with finding any items they may be looking for
- Supported Reference and Children Department Librarians and Associates in finding items
- Attended annual page meetings for updated procedures and customer service policies

OTHER EXPERIENCE

Sunshine Senior Living   2012 – 2014
Activities Assistant
- Volunteered at organization's retirement homes, assisting with computer literacy development of residents
- Attended community outreach for the organization, including community fairs, service club meetings and volunteer recruitment fairs
- Created new online system for scheduling and tracking activities calendars

CITATIONS

CHAPTER 2

www.theladders.com/career-advice/you-only-get-6-seconds-of-fame-make-it-count

www.themuse.com/advice/the-1-thing-hiring-managers-are-looking-for

www.businessinsider.com/resume-length-two-pages-or-one-2018-11

Chiaravalle, Bill and Barbara Findlay Schenk, *Branding for Dummies*, 2014

CHAPTER 4

https://hbr.org/2018/09/how-we-describe-male-and-female-job-applicants-differently

- Mikki Hebl
- Christine L. Nittrouer
- Abigail R. Corrington
- Juan M. Madera

https://hbr.org/2018/07/why-women-volunteer-for-tasks-that-dont-lead-to-promotions

- Maria P. Recalde
- Lise Vesterlund

DiGeronimo, JJ, *Accelerate Your Impact: Action-Based Strategies to Pave Your Professional Path*, 2016 (Cleveland, Ohio: Smart Business Books)

CATHY'S FAVORITE RESOURCES FOR RESUME DEVELOPMENT AND CAREER INSPIRATION

BOOKS

Resumes for Dummies (7th edition) by Laura DeCarlo (For Dummies, 2015)

Resume Magic: Trade Secrets of a Professional Resume Writer (4th edition) by Susan Britton Whitcomb (Jist Works, 2010)

Career Match: Connecting Who You Are with What You'll Love to Do by Shoya Zichy with Ann Bidou (AMACOM, 2007)

The Pathfinder: How to Choose or Change Your Career for a Lifetime of Satisfaction and Success by Nicholas Lore (Fireside, 1998)

I Could Do Anything If Only I Knew What It Was: How to Discover What You Really Want and How to Get It by Barbara Sher (Dell, 1995)

Your Heart's Desire: Instructions for Creating the Life You Really Want by Sonia Choquette (Three Rivers Press, 1997)

ONLINE

The Muse – www.TheMuse.com

Forbes Magazine online – www.forbes.com (search "career" on the home page for most viewed career-related articles)

National Career Development Association – www.ncda.org (choose the Resources tab on the home page)

www.TechSavvyWomen.net

www.GlassDoor.com

ABOUT THE AUTHOR

Coach, speaker, trainer, and author, Cathy Posner is Founder and Principal at Transition Consulting and Coaching. After many years of working in HR, program development, and leadership for other organizations while consulting on the side, Cathy decided to give coaching her full attention. With her two-year-old daughter in tow, she launched her practice. Cathy provides career coaching, small business development, HR support, nonprofit consulting services, and workshops to transitioning individuals and organizations looking to grow or improve their processes. She also works as a Senior Coach with CareerCurve, providing outplacement and transition support to candidates, and as a training consultant, working to help companies improve their workplace communications and overall effectiveness. Cathy is very active in her northeast Ohio community and serves on a number of nonprofit boards and committees. Cathy was honored as a 2014 Woman of Professional Excellence through Women's Network of Northeast Ohio, was a 2018 Women of Our Community award recipient, and Athena Award nominee in Medina County, Ohio.

Cathy especially enjoys helping individuals and organizations connect with the things they are good at, and supporting each to develop those gifts.

CATHY'S COACHING AND SPEAKING SERVICES

Cathy can help you or your organization! She works across a diverse array of industries and job titles.

She offers career coaching, transition or promotion coaching, business coaching, team coaching, Human Resources support services, and nonprofit organization coaching. Services include resume writing, career mapping assistance, goal setting, and organizational assessments to increase efficiency or effectiveness.

Cathy can also bring fresh perspective, direction, and inspiration to your team or group. She offers engaging, interactive, and informative presentations on a number of topics, from how to brand yourself on LinkedIn; to communicating with impact, clarity and emotional intelligence; to building a more effective leadership team.

To learn more about how Cathy can *help you see the possibilities,* contact her via*:*

Phone	216-337-2106
Website	www.TransitionConsultingAndCoaching.com
Email	Cathy@TransitionConsultingAndCoaching.com
LinkedIn	www.linkedin.com/in/CathyPosner/
Facebook	@TransitionConsultingAndCoachingCathyPosner

Acknowledgments

Peg and Lloyd, my parents, you never put any limits on my thinking about what I could be and what I could do—in fact, you've encouraged me in countless ways at every turn my career has taken.

Mason, you have been my support, champion, and partner in all things. I recently read this quote by Michelle Obama and thought of you: "My marriage to Barack gave me the courage to explore what would bring me joy." Although I've never shied away from joyful choices, having you by my side has made them all the richer.

Lucinda, it is so cool to hear your daughter talk about how proud she is that her mom is an author. I love talking about work projects (and everything else!) with you and take your opinions to heart. Always.

Bonnie, what can I say? What started as an accidental attendance at your session at the Regional ICF conference sparked a year-long project and professional relationship for many years to come. You are so very good at what you do! Thank you for helping me achieve this goal.

JJ, our conversations are always fast and on the fly but packed with good ideas. I love that you always ask, "What if you …?" That takes my ideas in new directions.

40900252R00050

Made in the USA
Lexington, KY
03 June 2019